Sister
IMAGES

Mary Zimmer

ABINGDON PRESS / Nashville

SISTER IMAGES

Copyright © 1993 by Abingdon Press

This book is printed on recycled, acid-free paper.

Library of Congress Cataloging–in–Publication Data

Zimmer, Mary, 1947–
  Sister images / Mary Zimmer.
    p.   cm.
  ISBN 0-687-38556-3 (alk. paper)
  1. Women in the Bible.   2. Women—Prayer-books and devotions.   3. Meditations.   I. Title.
BS575.Z56   1993
220.9'2'082—dc10   93–18259
                                                        CIP

Scripture quotations, unless otherwise noted, are from the New Revised Standard Version Bible, Copyright © 1989 by the Division of Christian Education of the National Council of the Churches of Christ in the USA. Used by permission.

Scripture quotations noted NEB are from *The New English Bible.* © The Delegates of the Oxford University Press and The Syndics of the Cambridge University Press 1961, 1970. Reprinted by permission.

93 94 95 96 97 98 99 00 01 02 — 10 9 8 7 6 5 4 3 2 1

MANUFACTURED IN THE UNITED STATES OF AMERICA

This book is dedicated to
Lynn Barnes Hamilton
and
Carole Barnes Higgins
Sisters of the womb by chance
Sisters of the heart by choice

Acknowledgments

November 21, 1992—Writing acknowledgments on the Saturday before Thanksgiving is an excellent spiritual discipline. These words are a beginning hint of the gratitude I feel for the persons listed here.

A book of six years' gestation has a number of midwives. I would like to thank:

Steve Shoemaker, pastor, friend, and brother, whose constant trustworthiness and belief in me have been living, breathing grace.

Molly Marshall, sister in faith and life, whose teaching challenges me and whose empathy nourishes me.

Bill Rogers and Bill Johnson, teachers and ministers who call me colleague and provide vibrant, steadfast compassion.

Loyd Allen for saying, "Why don't you go see this editor from Abingdon?" and Glenn Hinson for starting me on this pilgrimage called ministry when he looked me in the eye and said, "Follow Jesus."

Elaine Prevalete and the Sisters of Loretto for a place of retreat that has been a womb for words.

Bill Thomason, who provided generous consults and referrals for both writing and publishing.

Leslie Kendrick, Laura Lea Duckworth, Jane Parker, and others in the Friday morning Spirituality Group whose affirmation and empowerment are so crucial to creativity and the "writing life."

Pat Chervenak, a warm, kind spiritual director who kept asking, "And where is God in this?"

Reba Cobb and Rev. Christi Schmidt, and other women in ministry who say, "Yes, I understand. Keep pushing."

Women encouragers of Crescent Hill Baptist Church, like Mildred Burch, Elaine Parker, Margaret Graves, and Betty Cook, who once said, "Mary, why don't you do the meditations for the women's retreat?"

Solidarity Sunday School Class of Crescent Hill Baptist Church because they are friends who are family.

Roxann and Bob Hieb and Diane and Rae Taylor whose suppers and love, laughter and hugs, keep me grounded.

June Hobbs and Bobbie Thomason, strong and steadfast sisters of my heart, who grieve with me when I cry, whose giggles nurture me, and whose long talks inspire me to keep going—and to keep writing.

And, of course, my deep gratitude to the men in my life—my younger son, Michael, who brings cherry pops, bubble gum, and hugs to a mother who spends many hours in a study. And Jacob, whose groaner puns, jokes, and creative questions lighten my heart. And my husband and friend, Steve, who wonders lovingly about a woman who writes down everything she thinks, but whose generous support buys a desk, computer, and file cabinet so she can, and whose rock-ribbed love has surrounded me for twenty-four years.

Contents

Preface 9

1. *Introduction*—Guided Imagery Meditation 13

Sisters of Wisdom

2. *Miriam*—Making Connections 19

3. *Huldah*—Sharing Wisdom 25

4. *Deborah*—Choosing Battles 31

5. *Woman with Costly Perfume*—What Is Your Gift? 37

Sisters of Strife

6. *The Samaritan Woman*—Living Water 43

7. *Mary of Bethany*—Choosing the Better Part 51

8. *The Bent-over Woman*—What Needs Healing? 55

9. *The Woman Taken in Adultery*—Blessing and Forgiveness 61

Sisters of Faith

10. *Hannah*—Making a Sacrifice 69

11. *Martha*—Faith Beyond Grief 75

12. *Mary Magdalene*—Called to Proclaim 81

13. *Lydia, Priscilla, and Phoebe*—Steadfast Women 87

Sisters of Woe

14. *Eve*—Necessary Temptation 95

15. *Hagar*—God's Comfort and Protection 101

16. *Sarah*—Victimized by Another's Fear 107

17. *Daughter of Jephthah*—Pride and Pain 113

Sisters of Courage

18. *Shiphrah and Puah*—Courageous Creation 121

19. *Ruth*—Courage to Risk 127

20. *Mary, the Mother of Jesus*—The Hardest Words 133

21. *The Canaanite Woman*—Getting Needs Met 139

Preface

Multicolored balloons—red, blue, yellow, and green—floated off into a gray, autumn sky past the front portico of the cathedral. Below me, rows of white crosses marked the graves of Catholic sisters, who had searched for God from their quiet convent above a small, Indiana town. Behind me were my Baptist sisters. We had been making the same search on our annual retreat.

I turned to look at my friends' faces. Some were solemn as they moved to head home. Some exchanged smiles and quiet talk. Others wept as they shared hugs.

And I wondered about all the times women had gotten together to search for and serve God. I thought of Miriam, who made connections near a riverbank, and Ruth, who committed herself to Naomi, and the company of steadfast women in the early churches.

By June, 1984 had already been a hard year and I went to the Sisters of Loretto Motherhouse in Nerinx, Kentucky, for the relief of a personal retreat. Beside a calm, green lake rimmed by huge trees, I sat to ponder the pain of violated trust and battered self-image. I spent time in a small, intimate library and searched for comfort in classics of meditation. Instead, I discovered my sisters—Hagar, who fled to the desert, and the bent-over woman healed on the Sabbath despite the authorities' protest.

🪶

On Sunday evenings a few of us gathered to work on *Folio*, a journal for Southern Baptist women in ministry. In our upper room crowded with two desks, files, and just enough chairs, we met on this particular night to mourn. The Southern Baptist Convention, rent by rumor and conflict, had passed a resolution that women should not be ordained because they represented Eve who "brought evil into the world." A story of one bite of forbidden fruit and women have been condemned ever since to second-class status before God and in the church.

And I remembered the daughter of Jephthah who was sacrificed for her father's bargain with God, and Mary Magdalene who persevered and proclaimed Christ's message.

🪶

It had been one of those days when my multiple roles and endless tasks tumbled around in my confused head. The phone rang every half hour. My sons needed help with their projects. And I vowed to escape to the library after dinner.

The library was quiet as I began my search. I picked out several traditional devotional books. They just didn't fit. Then I saw a book with a full-color photo of a dandelion on it. Who would put a weed on the front of a devotional book?

The book was *Opening to God* by Carolyn Stahl. Ms. Stahl offered a different kind of devotion, called "guided imagery meditation." As I read, the words broke my assumed familiarity with the texts. Images like the seed and the vine, and characters like Mary and Martha became immediate and vibrant.

I realized that the help my sisters and I needed was available in the stories and spirit of our biblical sisters. And the method that could make that help available to us is guided imagery meditation.

Another retreat and another cemetery. This one lies at the end of a path along the Stations of the Cross at Nerinx. There is a simple black iron fence with a gate. Two enormous stone angels stand just inside. The arms of each are stretched out in welcome.

And suddenly I sense the presence of my biblical sisters—the women of the Bible. Their spirits are stretched out to us like the open arms of angels. They offer their stories, their pain and triumph, and their joys to us. We can, with open hearts, receive and learn from them.

1
Introduction
Guided Imagery Meditation

Carolyn Stahl writes, "We have access to Divine Guidance through intuition, creativity and a sense of unity with the world, but we do not always use our imagination" (*Opening to God*, Nashville: The Upper Room, 1977). Imagination is a gift we have all been given. It is the source of human creativity. Unfortunately, it is not always valued, and sometimes a child's imagination is disparaged as "telling stories" or punished as "lying." And many adults leave behind their imaginations as they grow older and get busy with career, home, and family.

Perhaps you have over-controlled your imagination and intuition in the service of other important aspects of your life. But your imagination is still with you and can be developed with patience and practice. These meditations are designed to be opportunities to use your imagination as an avenue to your inner self. That deep, still part can be opened to a loving God who is always there and always waiting.

Guided imagery meditation is a method that uses imagination as a tool to focus our senses on a particular image or series of images in a church service or in personal, contemplative prayer. In these meditations, the basic scene and elements of the biblical woman's life are recreated in a way that allows us to feel ourselves confronted by God and gives us an opportunity to respond.

In both the Hebrew Scriptures and the Christian Scriptures, there are many stories that use symbols, dreams, and images to develop the message. Jesus' parables usually contained an extended metaphor through which the meaning of the story grows and deepens as the parable is studied.

The symbols and images in these meditations can be used in the same way. By concentrating on what may be an under-utilized part of our God-given selves, we can find new and rewarding paths of spiritual growth and the always welcome sense that we are not here alone—our biblical sisters have been here before us. The spirit contained in their stories is available to inspire and counsel us in our contemporary struggles.

Guided imagery meditation is a means of opening our spirituality to a new experience of what God might be in our lives. But the purpose of these meditations is not restricted to withdrawal from the world in order to seek communion with God. It is just as important to move out *into* the world with the insights and purposes gained from meditation.

USING THIS BOOK

The meditations are divided into four parts. The scripture base is included so that you have the story at hand. The second section is interpretive commentary with emphasis on reflections and implications that may be new to you. That is followed by a guided imagery meditation with minimal instructions. Finally, there is a short, concluding prayer.

These meditations can be psychologically powerful because they are intentionally written to reach parts of the self that we may not usually notice or that we may purposefully hide from our everyday consciousness. For this reason, the power can be beneficial, or, in times of stress, it can be uncomfortable. Personal choice about level of depth or vulnerability you bring to the meditations is encouraged.

The newness of this method may feel uncomfortable at first, particularly if you have no experience with silent or focused meditation. There are several methods that may help. You might simply read through the chapter and write your reactions to the commentary and the meditation. You might want to read the meditations into a tape recorder and play them back for yourself.

If you are in a prayer study group or have a prayer partner, spend some time with this book by taking turns reading the meditations aloud to one another. The book can be utilized as devotionals in Sunday school classes, study groups, and discipleship and mission groups.

All experienced practitioners of meditation use various methods of preparation. Certain physical aspects of the body are important. One is posture. The best posture is to be seated in a firm chair that supports the back. Both feet can rest on the floor. Your body, hands, and face should be relaxed. I often find that my impulse is to have my hands open upward. All of these instructions are intended to create a posture in which your body shows its readiness to be open to the experience. You should feel physically comfortable and supported, yet alert. Closing your eyes helps.

The other important method of preparation is breathing. Most meditation practices use controlled breathing because it is a natural body rhythm that we can pay attention to and control. The meditations in the book begin with some phrase that indicates this process. Basically, it is a slow, deep breathing, which, after practice, signals your body and mind that it is time to begin.

Do not be discouraged. Finding your own posture and relaxed breathing rhythm may take some time. Try different chairs, different means of relaxation and breathing until you find the right combination for you.

Most people who have learned and follow a method of Christian meditation consider it a means of significant spiritual growth. Any method of meditation is also a method of personal discipline. Learning one requires openness to new experience and takes practice. It is my hope that these meditations provide you with an expanded life of prayer as you reflect on the lives of biblical women and as you experience God's word to you in the images of their stories.

Sisters of Wisdom

2

Miriam
Making Connections

Now a man from the house of Levi went and married a Levite woman. The woman conceived and bore a son; and when she saw that he was a fine baby, she hid him three months. When she could hide him no longer she got a papyrus basket for him, and plastered it with bitumen and pitch; she put the child in it and placed it among the reeds on the bank of the river. His sister stood at a distance, to see what would happen to him.

The daughter of Pharaoh came down to bathe at the river, while her attendants walked beside the river. She saw the basket among the reeds and sent her maid to bring it. When she opened it, she saw the child. He was crying, and she took pity on him, "This must be one of the Hebrews' children," she said. Then his sister said to Pharaoh's daughter, "Shall I go and get you a nurse from the Hebrew women to nurse the child for you?" Pharaoh's daughter said to her, "Yes." So the girl went and called the child's mother. Pharaoh's daughter said to her, "Take this child and nurse it for me, and I will give you your wages." So the woman took the child and nursed it. When the child grew up, she brought him to Pharaoh's daughter, and she took him as her son. She named him Moses, "because," she said, "I drew him out of the water." **(Exodus 2:1-10)**

The courtroom was quiet and smaller than I expected. There were no observers, just my parents and their lawyer, my sisters and I and our lawyer, and the judge and court reporter. We were there for a petition assigning guardianship of my parents and their affairs to my sisters and me. Because of their deteriorating capacities and several scary incidents, we would assume the legal and moral responsibility of their lives. It was a new kind of sisterhood, one we have to handle with honesty, tact, and much communication, one we would never have chosen.

Sisterhood is one of those words we didn't grow up hearing, though we may have lived it out with our biological sisters, our childhood girlfriends, Girl Scout troop, or school friends. We might have grown up with one model—aunts, mothers, and grandmothers in the kitchen cooking and cleaning for a family meal. They shared recipes, passed on advice about children and men, and teased and argued about different approaches to the two or three roles they fulfilled.

But in our contemporary lives of many roles, there may be several kinds of sisterhood we create. Single mothers form support groups for potluck suppers. A mom working outside the home develops a close friendship with her child's day care teacher. A single woman joins a networking group for career support. Retired women may plan leisure activities or volunteer work together. A Sunday school class or mission group can function as sisterhood for its members. Women with a burden for justice form activist groups around a specific social or political agenda. The women's movement began and flourished in such "consciousness-raising" groups.

The sisterhood model is inherently one of equality and mutuality. There are no supervisors, presidents, or chairpersons, no bishops or presbyters. The operating principle is that all participate with different, but equal gifts. Leadership and responsibility are shared. Does the idea ring a bell?

Any group that becomes sisterhood starts because one or more women recognize a mutual need. Reaching out to one another begins sisterhood and keeps it growing. Sometimes sisterhood is planned and organized. Other times it happens spontaneously around a specific occasion.

The story of young Miriam is one of the latter. Most of us have heard this passage as the story of baby Moses in the basket. It is not often taught to adults. But look at the story again and concentrate on the women, particularly young Miriam. Moses' mother defies the Pharaoh and nurtures her infant son for a few months. Then when he is three months old, she hides him in a basket and Miriam "stood at a distance, to see what would happen to him." When Pharaoh's daughter notices the basket and finds the baby, Miriam steps out of her hiding place, asserts herself by offering to find a nurse for the baby, and goes to get her mother.

Sister Miriam is loyal, astute, and courageous in this story. First she stands to watch. Then at just the right moment, she steps out and speaks. Her act here is the one that creates all the connections between the women who will make it possible for Moses to live. It takes them all—a natural mother to feed him and a powerful adoptive mother who will raise him to adulthood and a place in the world. And young Miriam, by her quick and keen judgment, integrates the two worlds that are otherwise separate.

Think of the context of this story. Miriam's family—indeed her whole people—are slaves. Out of fear of their numbers, the Pharaoh has enslaved them, set them to oppressive and dehumanizing labor, and embarked on a course of genocide to decrease their numbers. With Shiphrah and Puah, Miriam defies the ruling order. She does not run away when Pharaoh's daughter approaches. She responds to the woman's compassion by establishing a temporary sisterhood, a connection between these women. And she does it in the face of slavery.

It seems a minor action, just one question: "Shall I go to get you a nurse?" It is not dramatic; it will not free her people from slavery for many years. But it is the precipitous event, because her assertive words save into an unknown future the life of one brother who will lead the people out of slavery. This connection creates a serendipitous sisterhood that saves the life of an infant whom the overpowering structures of dominance would murder.

Miriam has learned how to take calculated risks from a mother who takes a chance by handing over a tiny infant to a river. Like Hannah later, Jochebed gives up her son. She takes a chance that in the river in a basket, he will at least survive drowning by the Pharaoh's soldiers. Miriam is set to watch. These women have virtually no power in their society. They are slaves. Like Shiphrah and Puah, the only power they have is their cunning and courage.

I believe the story comes down to us like this for a reason. The story of Miriam signifies (as others in the Bible do) that it is often the connections between women that further God's purposes in human life. In the stories of Ruth and Naomi, and Mary and Elizabeth, it is the commonality of their needs that brings them together. They recognize and acknowledge one another's struggle and one another's integrity.

At one time or another, each of us fills each of the roles in this story. We have been enslaved by someone else's fear. Each of us has been the maidservant because in every need or ministry, somebody has to wade into the muddy water to pick up the basket. And just as the maidservant isn't named, so we also may have missed out on any credit. We have some of the resources and the compassion of Pharaoh's daughter, or we wouldn't be in this life-style called *Christian*. We are often set to watch over someone or something as vulnerable as a baby floating in a basket in a river. Then we, too, must step out, ask the question or make the proclamation that establishes a connection that defies enslavement and stakes a claim for freedom.

Reaching out to create and maintain sisterhood is also a matter of priority. If we can put the activities of our sisterhood near the top of our list, then we are also taking care of the sometimes neglected person inside. She is one who needs affirmation of her experience and who needs support from another sister or brother who really understands.

GUIDED IMAGERY MEDITATION

Find a comfortable, alert position. . . . Close your eyes and begin a process of deep, slow breathing. . . .

Imagine it is a hot day. . . . The sun is pouring down on your back and shoulders. . . . Feel the heat. . . .

You are standing just at the edge of the river. . . . What does the scene look like? . . . Look at the sky, . . . the trees, . . . the water. . . . Notice a basket in the water. . . . It floats on the rippling water. . . .

You become aware that you are responsible for this basket. . . . There is someone or something that is very vulnerable and you must be protective. . . .

What is the responsibility you carry? . . . Imagine a symbol of it in the basket. . . .

Watch . . . and . . . wait. . . .

Now think of others who might help you carry out this responsibility. . . . Who can support you in your task? . . . What connections do you need to make to get the support you need? . . .

Imagine yourself reaching out. . . . Seeking the people and resources that will help you. . . . What must you say? . . .

Dear God,

We have many baskets in our lives—many tasks and responsibilities that we watch over. Forgive our impatience. Help us to know that we don't have to carry it alone. Grant us insight and energy to step out and make connections with our sisters that lighten our burdens and further your purpose on earth. Amen.

3

Huldah
Sharing Wisdom

The high priest Hilkiah said to Shaphan the secretary, "I have found the book of the law in the house of the LORD." When Hilkiah gave the book to Shaphan, he read it. Then Shaphan the secretary came to the king, and reported to the king, "Your servants have emptied out the money that was found in the house, and have delivered it into the hand of the workers who have oversight of the house of the LORD." Shaphan the secretary informed the king, "The priest Hilkiah has given me a book." Shaphan then read it aloud to the king.

When the king heard the words of the book of the law, he tore his clothes. Then the king commanded the priest Hilkiah, Ahikam son of Shaphan, Achbor son of Micaiah, Shaphan the secretary, and the king's servant Asaiah, saying, "Go, inquire of the LORD for me, for the people, and for all Judah, concerning the words of this book that has been found; for great is the wrath of the LORD that is kindled against us, because our ancestors did not obey the words of this book, to do according to all that is written concerning us."

So the priest Hilkiah, Ahikam, Achbor, Shaphan, and Asaiah went to the prophetess Huldah the wife of Shallum son of Tikvah, son of Harhas, keeper of the wardrobe; she resided in Jerusalem in the Second Quarter, where they consulted her. She declared to them, "Thus says the LORD, the God of Israel: Tell the man who sent you to me, Thus says the LORD, I will indeed bring disaster on this place and on its inhabitants—all the words of the book that the king of Judah has read. Because they have abandoned me and have made offerings to other gods, so that they have provoked me to anger with all the work of their hands, therefore my wrath will be kindled against this place, and it will not be quenched. But as to the king of Judah, who sent you to inquire of the LORD, thus shall you say to him, Thus says the LORD, the God of Israel: Regarding the words that you have heard, because your heart was penitent, and you humbled yourself before the LORD, when you heard how I spoke against this place, and against its inhabitants, that they should become a desolation and a curse, and because you have torn your clothes and wept before me, I also have heard you, says the LORD. Therefore, I will gather you to your ancestors, and you shall be gathered to your grave in peace; your eyes shall not see all the disaster that I will bring on this place." They took the message back to the king.   **(2 Kings 22:8-20)**

*T*he assignment in my seminary class was to consider my own personal power and authority. When did I feel powerful and authoritative? What do I do with my power? How should it be used in ministry and in the church? I'd never heard the questions stated in just that way, with the assumption that I had a right to power and authority and a requisite responsibility for their use. Certainly the concepts of free will and the priesthood of the believer fit in with having personal power and authority. But what about servanthood? What is the power of the Christian and minister who seek to live out of the kingdom idea that the first shall be last? I thought of the story of Huldah.

"Huldah?" my friend and seminary Ph.D. graduate said. "I've heard the name somewhere." Perhaps the story of this prophetess has been lost in the larger story of King Josiah. Perhaps the injunction in 1 Timothy became a retroactive blanket thrown over the stories of women in the Bible so that those women who were not silent were silenced. Whatever the reason, Huldah is, along with the daughter of Jephthah, Tamar, and others, one of the lost women of the Bible, unknown to many who have spent their lives in the church.

The story of Huldah and Josiah, like that of Deborah and Barak, turns the traditional roles inside out. King Josiah is distraught with panic when he hears the words of the book found in the Temple. He sends his officers and priests to seek the Lord's guidance "for the people and for all Judah."

Why do they go to Huldah? We are not given any information about her reputation, but it must have been extensive since the highest officials of the land seek her. Surely it is significant that they go to her, rather than send for her. This might be one sign that the wisdom of her prophecies was well known. Her social status is likely not very important; based on the information given, she is the wife of the grandson of the king's servant. But her charisma, her gift of prophecy must have been recognized, for it is to this lowly woman of "the Second Quarter" that the leaders go in order to seek the Lord's guidance.

Another sign of the validity of Huldah as a prophet is the repetition of the prophetic formula: "Thus says the LORD." The use of the formula marks Huldah's status as a recognized authority to interpret the will of the Lord. The themes of Huldah's interpretation are consistent with those of the major prophets: Yahweh will forsake the chosen people because they have forsaken God and worshiped other gods, "the work of their hands."

This is another story in which what we are not told is significant. Huldah is not shy and self-effacing. She does not marvel that her wisdom is sought or make self-deprecating remarks. The implication is that she has confidence in the prophecy God gives her and she speaks with candor. She responds out of the wisdom that has been given to her when her gift of foresight is needed.

The consequences of her prophecy go far beyond the assumed influence of a woman in the patriarchal society. Only after he has the confirmation of Huldah's interpretation does Josiah proceed with the reforms for which he is acclaimed in the Old Testament. Josiah reads the book of the covenant in the Temple for all the people to hear. And then he commands that the Temple be cleansed of all idols to the other gods. He conducts a similar purge throughout Judah, changes the face of religion in Judah, and does all he can to reconcile his people to God.

There are four other women referred to as prophetesses in the Bible—Miriam, Deborah, Isaiah's wife, and Anna. In addition there are three women referred to as "wise women" in the Old Testament. Besides Deborah, Huldah is the only prophetess given significant reporting of what she says. It is very significant, in a primitive culture where much history was first told by word of mouth, that we even have the story of Huldah. The fact that her story made it into the history of the Kings is amazing. The other significant fact, in view of the larger history of the Israelites, is that the first person who is sought for interpretation of scripture is a woman. These facts and Huldah's story need to be brought out of the silent past.

Perhaps you know other Huldahs. Every church community has its Huldahs. They are the women leaders who are sought out for their opinions on crucial issues. Often they are not those with high visibility or status. But their wisdom is recognized; their perceptions about the right course of action is respected. If they are kept in silence and ignored, the church is in danger of losing the gifts of their wisdom and insight.

Perhaps you have been a Huldah for someone. Your personal power and authority have been recognized when someone seeks your opinion on a private or public matter. If you have spent your life in the "second quarter" of the church, you have observations and recommendations that the church needs for direction.

We may never be visited by national political and religious leaders for our prophecy, but as women created in the image of God, each one of us has the right to personal power and authority. We have the wisdom of our own life experiences and prayer. The world presents us with crucial issues that require our response. We have the responsibility to thoughtfully and tactfully address them. The time for quiet passivity is past.

The message of our sister Huldah is "Speak up. Write letters. Share your insights and wisdom." And the consequences of doing so may go farther and have greater impact than we can begin to imagine.

GUIDED IMAGERY MEDITATION

Begin taking a few deep breaths. . . . Breath deeply and slowly. . . .

Imagine you are settled at home. . . . You are working on a quiet chore. . . . There is a situation in your life. . . . It may be family . . . work . . . church . . . community. . . . It is unsettling . . . worrisome to you. . . . What is it? . . .

A knock comes at the door. . . . When you answer it several people are there. . . . They are leaders . . . powerful people in your life. . . .

They have come for your opinion . . . for your advice. . . . They say your wisdom is needed. . . .

From a deep, quiet place within you, there comes a sense of the right direction . . . the right course to take. . . . What do you say? . . . What is your inspiration? . . .

Dear God,

Somehow many of us have grown to adulthood believing we are not intelligent, experienced, or wise enough to give our opinion and share our insight. We passively wait for leaders to solve every problem. Keep us aware that each of us has something to offer—a personal wisdom different from anyone else's. And we can never know what influence we might have unless we speak up in the spirit of Christian love. Give us courage to share what you have revealed to us. Amen.

4
Deborah
Choosing Battles

Then the Israelites cried out to the LORD for help; for he [Sisera] had nine hundred chariots of iron, and had oppressed the Israelites cruelly twenty years.

At that time Deborah, a prophetess, wife of Lappidoth, was judging Israel. She used to sit under the palm of Deborah between Ramah and Bethel in the hill country of Ephraim; and the Israelites came up to her for judgment. She sent and summoned Barak son of Abinoam from Kedesh in Naphtali, and said to him, "The LORD, the God of Israel, commands you, 'Go, take position at Mount Tabor, bringing ten thousand from the tribe of Naphtali and the tribe of Zebulun. I will draw out Sisera, the general of Jabin's army, to meet you by the Wadi Kishon with his chariots and his troops; and I will give him into your hand.'" Barak said to her, "If you will go with me, I will go; but if you will not go with me, I will not go." And she said, "I will surely go with you; nevertheless, the road on which you are going will not lead to your glory, for the LORD will sell Sisera into the hand of a woman." Then Deborah got up and went with Barak to Kedesh. Barak summoned Zebulun and Naphtali to Kedesh; and ten thousand warriors went up behind him; and Deborah went up with him.

Now Heber the Kenite had separated from the other Kenites, that is, the descendants of Hobab the father-in-law of Moses, and had encamped as far away as Elon-bezaanannim, which is near Kedesh.

Then Deborah said to Barak, "Up! For this is the day on which the LORD has given Sisera into your hand. The LORD is indeed going out before you." So Barak went down from Mount Tabor with ten thousand warriors following him. And the LORD threw Sisera and all his chariots and all his army into a panic before Barak; Sisera got down from his chariot and fled away on foot, while Barak pursued the chariots and the army to Harosheth-ha-goiim. All the army of Sisera fell by the sword; no one was left.

Now Sisera had fled away on foot to the tent of Jael wife of Heber the Kenite; for there was peace between King Jabin of Hazor and the clan of

Heber the Kenite. Jael came out to meet Sisera, and said to him, "Turn aside, my lord, turn aside to me; have no fear." So he turned aside to her into the tent, and she covered him with a rug. Then he said to her, "Please give me a little water to drink; for I am thirsty." So she opened a skin of milk and gave him a drink and covered him. He said to her, "Stand at the entrance of the tent, and if anybody comes and asks you, 'Is anyone here?' say, 'No.'" But Jael wife of Heber took a tent peg, and took a hammer in her hand, and went softly to him and drove the peg into his temple, until it went down into the ground—he was lying fast asleep from weariness—and he died. Then, as Barak came in pursuit of Sisera, Jael went out to meet him, and said to him, "Come, and I will show you the man whom you are seeking." So he went into her tent; and there was Sisera lying dead, with the tent peg in his temple.

(Judges 4:3-11, 14-22)

A younger-than-middle-aged woman stands in her perfect silk suit with every hair in place. Her makeup and a little airbrushing eliminate any flaws. In one hand is a gleaming leather briefcase and curled in the other arm is the most adorable toddler you have ever seen in designer overalls and Weeboks.

This is the picture of superwoman brought to you by Madison Avenue. Inside the magazine there is an article about how this wonder-woman organized her day in order to have fresh crabmeat crepes on the table by six and a not-very-hostile takeover merger signed by noon the next day.

I never met one of those women who could work full-time in a demanding job, mother young children, and get through a whole week without take-out Chinese food *and* pizza.

Deborah had a palm tree rather than a briefcase. And though we are not told explicitly, a woman who had attained the designation of prophet was probably past her time of childbearing. It is curious that in her song, the only role Deborah refers to is that of mother: "you arose, Deborah, arose as a mother in Israel" (Judges 5:7a). She is the best candidate for superwoman in the

Old Testament, carrying the multiple roles of mother, judge, and prophet.

And Deborah is unique among the women of the Bible. She holds and exerts both political and spiritual power. The celebratory Song of Deborah is one of the oldest texts of the Bible; her story and song were so significant to the Israelites that they were preserved for thousands of years.

The tone of the story conveys Deborah's confidence in herself. That confidence has a social and political base since judges were elected by the people of Israel, and she is the only female judge recorded. Her spiritual wisdom as a prophet enhanced her role as judge. When the people determined to seek justice for their oppression, they went to Deborah and she did not fail them.

Deborah's first words in the passage are words from God; she announces a call from God to gather two tribes for a battle. The announcement contains a promise that the Israelites will be delivered.

But when Deborah announces the plan to Barak, we hear one of the most unusual responses in the Old Testament. We are not given a hint as to his motivation, but Barak refuses to obey the word of God unless the woman prophet goes with him. Does he doubt the prophecy and promise? Or is the internal situation such that the presence of the judge herself is required for warriors to go to battle?

Deborah's response seems to indicate the latter. She warns Barak that he will not be credited with the conquest of the enemy. There will be no personal glory in it for him. Instead Sisera will be conquered at the hands of a woman. But the woman is not Deborah herself.

As a prophet, Deborah's discernment is that the tribes will have to be called to unity in order to throw off the oppressor who enslaves them all. Barak then, and the Baraks in our lives, do not often make widespread changes in the lives of oppressed people without the prophetic discernment and wise counsel of women. Our awareness of our own oppression, of whatever kind and to whatever degree, should sensitize us to the oppression other women experience. Like Deborah, we have insight, wisdom, and the ability to persuade contemporary Baraks that battle must be joined to emancipate the oppressed.

On the day of battle, Deborah begins the action by rousing an apparently still-reluctant Barak. He wins the battle—an enormous one from the number of men and chariots—and spares none of his enemies. Sisera, the Canaanite general, flees into what at first appears to be a safe haven—the home of Heber the Kenite who did not go to war.

And we encounter Jael, a woman, whose name and part in the story have often been left out because of her brutal act. We have no hint of her shrewdness as she gives Sisera a place to rest, a drink, and appears to acquiesce in his request for protection.

Instinctive resistance is probably a natural response given the cultural dissonance between primitive Israelites and ourselves. But Jael was a woman of the tents, a member of the nomadic tribes, and as women were responsible for the assembly of the tents, she would have the skill to murder with one blow.

In our day, we no longer encounter, except by accident, the situation that Jael did. But due to Sisera's cowardice in running from the battle, she had the chance to rid the Israelites of their oppressor with one act. We must view that act in the context of her life. Women isolated from community in ancient, medieval, and pioneer times, faced the choice of killing another to save children or other community members. Because these acts are antithetical to our stereotype of ideal womanhood, we either ignore them or remain appalled. Jael's story is the lesson to us that with whatever kind and amount of power we have, we occasionally hold the tent peg and mallet in our hand. And when we do, we face our own capacity for destruction and how we will deal with our oppressor.

We live in a world that is distant in time from Deborah's and Jael's. But our world also seems to be fascinated by, even to worship, power and violence at times. When family massacres in Texas and Iowa by angry men fill the news, we wonder at the capacity for violence and revenge in the human soul. When we consider Jael, we are forced to consider our own capacity for violence in both words and deeds.

Deborah and Jael took the strengths they each possessed, discerned what should be done and acted to release their people from oppression. As women today, we have two models in this story—Deborah as the interpreter and inspiration of her people and Jael as the pragmatic action-oriented person who is called in Deborah's Song "most blessed of tent-dwelling women." The result of Deborah and Jael's courage is that their land was at peace for forty years.

Deborah and Jael's example to women in the church today is a difficult one to conceive, much less carry out. But their story is there to inspire us. Most of us will never be elected a judge, but we have the power of judgment in issues that impact the lives of women, men, and children. And the world needs that judgment from women in the church. We may not publicly be named prophet, but we have both the individual and corporate power of discernment and wisdom. And the world needs widespread proclamation of the discernment and wisdom of women who share the revelation they have received from God.

We can determine who the Canaanites are in our own lives and in our communal life. For most of us the oppression is much more subtle than military might. But the first step in beginning a battle against oppression is naming it, and we can name the oppression that feels like nine hundred chariots of iron. We can find the Barak in our place and time who might not be likely to share the credit, but who needs persuasion on behalf of those we are called to release. Our discernment of the will of God and our judgment of the needed course of action are necessary steps to finding the courage and energy required to do battle with violence and oppression. Deborah and Jael stand beside us every step of the way and we can claim the promise given them: God will deliver you and the people.

GUIDED IMAGERY MEDITATION

Find a comfortable position that allows you to feel alert. . . . Begin taking several slow deep breaths.

You are sitting quietly under a tree. . . . It is morning. . . . You have not yet taken up the burdens of your day. . . . Watch the leaves in the wind. . . . Look at the land around you. . . . Look at the sky . . . and absorb its vastness. . . .

As you sit, you become aware of an image of oppression that you know of in your life or another's . . . This is the nine hundred chariots of iron. . . . Name the oppression. . . .

Think for a moment about how this oppression feels. . . . Do you sense fear? . . . anger? . . . a numb passivity?

What is your judgment about this oppression? . . . What is the battle that must be fought? . . . What is your proclamation about the battle? . . .

Rouse yourself. . . . Rouse yourself to go out . . . to do battle against this oppression. . . . Do you need a Barak? . . . Name the Barak you will seek and persuade. . . .

Know that God will give you courage and strength. . . . God will give you strength like the sun rising in the morning. . . . The light of God's power will shine through all the day of battle. . . . Then the celebration will come. . . .

Dear God,

The power structures that impact our lives are so complex. And the experience of oppression is draining. There is seldom any time or energy left to fight for what we need and deserve. Keep Deborah and Jael in our hearts and minds that we may learn of their insight and courage. Keep us sensitized to the needs of those who live out their lives under oppression near and far. Inspire us to persevere in the cause of justice and mercy. Amen.

5
Woman with Costly Perfume
What Is Your Gift?

While he was at Bethany in the house of Simon the leper, as he sat at the table, a woman came with an alabaster jar of very costly ointment of nard, and she broke open the jar and poured the ointment on his head. But some were there who said to one another in anger, "Why was the ointment wasted in this way? For this ointment could have been sold for more than three hundred denarii, and the money given to the poor." And they scolded her. But Jesus said, "Let her alone; why do you trouble her? She has performed a good service for me. For you always have the poor with you, and you can show kindness to them whenever you wish; but you will not always have me. She has done what she could; she has anointed my body beforehand for its burial. Truly I tell you, wherever the good news is proclaimed in the whole world, what she has done will be told in remembrance of her." **(Mark 14:3-9)**

*I*n the movie *Babette's Feast*, based on the story by Isak Dinesen, a woman refugee is taken in by two devout sisters who care for a small religious group in a remote Scandinavian village. In exchange for room and board, she offers to keep house and cook. Soon after, she is notified of a winning lottery ticket. She offers to create a dinner for the anniversary of their father's death. The sisters agree and then fear that their own and the community's righteousness will be undermined by the luxury of the feast. The meal is a banquet of sumptuous tastes and smells. Afterwards the sisters talk with Babette about her return home. She tells them she will be staying on as their housekeeper because she has spent all the lottery winnings on the meal.

Babette and the woman with costly perfume are sisters of the spirit because they know that sometimes life calls us to the extravagant expression of our abilities and our love.

Those who scold the woman the apostle John calls Mary of Bethany, and the dedicated, compassionate sisters in Isak Dinesen's story are partners in their fear of extravagance. And I must confess, as a social worker, my first reaction used to be to side with the angry people in this story. "Why this waste?" And "the poor will always be with us?" Such a statement is oppressive and doesn't give the inspiration necessary to fight the barriers that poor people in our contemporary society face every day. But there is a lot more to this story than the traditional and mistaken justification for poverty in our world.

The larger context of this story in Mark's Gospel makes it a dramatic foreshadowing of Jesus' path to the cross. The most recent words of Jesus in the preceding chapter are the instructions to "keep alert" and "keep awake." The woman's actions show that she has learned this lesson. And the verses in chapter 14 just before the story describe the plot of priests and doctors of the law to seize Jesus. Just after this story is the note that Judas goes to the priests to betray his teacher. The woman's act is a prophetic one, but only Jesus recognizes this.

This is one of the many stories in the New Testament where Jesus focuses on and supports the behavior of a woman and rebukes the men who are criticizing her. He contrasts the sensitive awareness of this woman with their complacency. And look at the implications of this story.

Costly perfume is a wonderful symbol for spiritual gifts. This is not a paltry gift. It is expensive and luxurious. The woman is not cautious with her gift. She pours it out. Imagine pouring a full bottle of perfume all at once for someone you love.

The essence of perfume is ephemeral. It appeals to what in our sophisticated, plastic culture has become a minor sense. We don't rely on our sense of smell as Galilean villagers would have. An odor is often hard to define and, once released, cannot be contained again. Such is the Holy Spirit within us. And like the smell of perfume, we cannot control where it goes or how anyone else responds to it. Once extravagance of perfume or spirit is let loose, it goes where it will.

The criticism laid on the woman is not mild. Mark reports, "They turned upon her with fury" (Mark 14:5b NEB). Can't you just hear someone muttering, "hysterical female"? Perhaps one of the implications of this story is that in using our gifts for Christ we must have the courage to risk even the fury of other Christians in order to share our gifts with those who need them.

Then listen again to Jesus' defense and affirmation of the woman's actions. "Let her alone; why do you trouble her? She has performed a good service for me. . . . She has done what she could" (6:6, 8a).

What is the compulsion of these followers to criticize such an extravagant gift? The others present suffer from a tyranny of oughts based in law; but her gift is total and complete. She gives all, empties her perfume and her social standing by her intrusive act. Chances are, she will now become a member of the poor, just as Babette remained a housekeeper.

The economy they use to judge her is the standard one: what is considered usual in most cases. But her economy is transcendent. She only does one thing—breaks open a jar of perfume and anoints Jesus' head. But she also had to break through the crowd, break the social custom, and thereby she breaks their arrogant assumptions about what this time was and what was crucial at this moment.

This woman recognized that Jesus has his face set toward the cross, but the crowd does not. They think they are only having dinner. They are focused on exterior things; she has intuited the interior reality of Jesus and wants only to recognize this.

And her deepest intention is acknowledged by Jesus. He understands that she has done what only she can do, the act of personal power she chooses. His response to her gift of anointing and understanding is to make her a place in the gospel: wherever it is told, she will be remembered.

Hard as it is to imagine, this story is true for each of us. We have gifts of the Spirit that are contained within us. We can recognize the point at which they must be poured out extravagantly, regardless of the judgment of our society. For when those times come, we will also be anointing Jesus on his way to the cross.

The meditation that follows is an invitation to ponder your gifts and see what lies in your power.

GUIDED IMAGERY MEDITATION

Please find a comfortable, yet alert posture. Close your eyes and take a few deep breaths. . . .

Imagine you are seated in a room. . . . It is crowded with people . . . some you know . . . some are strangers. . . .

You hold in your hands a container. . . . Look at it. . . . Look at the color . . . the shape . . . the texture. . . . Take a moment to cherish the qualities of what you hold in your hand. . . .

Inside this container is your gift of the Spirit. . . . It is luxurious and precious . . . a worthy treasure. . . . Hold it up and smell the perfume. . . . What is it like? . . . Can you name your gift? . . .

There are people in the crowd who need and value your gift. . . . Who are they? . . . Where will you pour it out? . . .

You stand . . . ready to share your gift. . . . Others in the room turn to watch. . . . What do you do? . . . What lies in your power? . . .

Dear God,

We confess that sometimes fatigue makes us hoard our gifts. Sometimes envy makes us compare our gifts to others' instead of even considering pouring out our gifts.

Remind us that, like the woman in the story, sharing our gifts often requires sacrifice. Give us courage to make the sacrifice and the awareness that when we pour them out, we too, anoint Christ.

We remember that your grace is the source of our gifts. It is unlimited and we can seek your nurture when we are depleted. Amen.

Sisters of Strife

6

The Samaritan Woman
Living Water

A Samaritan woman came to draw water, and Jesus said to her, "Give me a drink." (His disciples had gone to the city to buy food.) The Samaritan woman said to him, "How is it that you, a Jew, ask a drink of me, a woman of Samaria?" (Jews do not share things in common with Samaritans.) Jesus answered her, "If you knew the gift of God, and who it is that is saying to you, 'Give me a drink,' you would have asked him, and he would have given you living water." The woman said to him, "Sir, you have no bucket, and the well is deep. Where do you get that living water? Are you greater than our ancestor Jacob, who gave us the well, and with his sons and his flocks drank from it?" Jesus said to her, "Everyone who drinks of this water will be thirsty again, but those who drink of the water that I will give them will never be thirsty. The water that I will give will become in them a spring of water gushing up to eternal life." The woman said to him, "Sir, give me this water, so that I may never be thirsty or have to keep coming here to draw water."

Jesus said to her, "Go, call your husband, and come back." The woman answered him, "I have no husband." Jesus said to her, "You are right in saying, 'I have no husband'; for you have had five husbands, and the one you have now is not your husband. What you have said is true!" The woman said to him, "Sir, I see that you are a prophet. Our ancestors worshiped on this mountain, but you say that the place where people must worship is in Jerusalem." Jesus said to her, "Woman, believe me, the hour is coming when you will worship the Father neither on this mountain nor in Jerusalem. You worship what you do not know; we worship what we know, for salvation is from the Jews. But the hour is coming, and is now here, when the true worshipers will worship the Father in spirit and truth, for the Father seeks such as these to worship him. God is spirit, and those who worship him must worship in spirit and truth." The woman said to him, "I know that Messiah is coming" (who is called Christ). "When he comes, he will proclaim all things to us." Jesus said to her, "I am he, the one who is speaking to you." Just then his disciples came. They were astonished that he was speaking with a woman, but no one said, "What do you want?" or, "Why are you speaking with her?" Then the woman left her water jar and went back to the city. She said to the people, "Come and see a man who told me everything I have ever done! He cannot be the Messiah, can he?"   **(John 4:7-29)**

There is a reservoir in my neighborhood that is part of the Louisville Water Company. I am one of the regular walkers around its perimeter. On the way back from my walk, I often sit by a fountain along Frankfort Avenue. When the morning or late afternoon sun hits the water drops, they sparkle with light. So the fountain has become an icon for me of the "inner spring of water always welling up" of which Jesus speaks in John 4. I go to the fountain to ask God the how and why questions of my life.

The Samaritan woman, or the woman at the well, was a woman of questions. She asked the socially taboo question of why Jesus, as a Jew, would speak to her, a Samaritan and a woman. She asked the pragmatic question about where Jesus might get a bucket for the promised living water. And by way of argument, she asked the theological question about where the spirit of God resides. The Samaritan woman has been judged as a cantankerous and stubborn person, but her persistent, even sarcastic, questions bring her to the realization that she is known by this man at the well. She finds her Messiah through her questions.

Her first response to Jesus' simple request for a drink is not a gracious one. She gets stuck in her surprise and discomfort at being accosted by this strange Jewish man. Jesus, in turn, immediately offers his unique spiritual gift by his response: "If you knew the gift of God," living water is possible. But she has no real inkling of what God gives. At this stage, her narrow, literal point of view prevents her from understanding the offer. How can someone without a bucket give water?

Don't we do the same? The evidence of God's blessings and

the chance for the living water of communion are all around us. And we are searching for buckets, so we can hold onto that living water and save it for later.

The woman confronts Jesus with the tradition of Jacob. The tangible water from this historical well means survival. How can he be more powerful or give her anything more crucial than that?

The spiritual theme of this passage is in Jesus' reply. He offers living water like a spring always welling up for eternity. But he is talking with a stubborn woman. She persists in her literal level; she can save time in her daily tasks if what he says is true.

There is energy in the Samaritan woman's questions. She has a seeking spirit and has argued long enough to find out that this man knows her whole truth. I have to admit I like her spunkiness. Maybe she's learned to persist because of a hard life with different men and the struggle to survive day by day. She confronts, argues, even defies this man who seems to speak so strangely.

But I wonder if Jesus doesn't get a little exasperated before he adopts the literal level of the woman. This stubborn woman requires some proof of his meaning and purpose and there's one way to do it. "Go, call your husband, and come back." She concedes that his knowledge of her life must mean that Jesus is a prophet.

So she sets up a theological debate: Well, then, explain why you worship in Jerusalem and we worship on the mountain. If he is a prophet he should have the answer to this age-old dilemma. It is still a valid question today with our plurality of denominations and different interpretations of Scripture.

As he often does, Jesus cuts through the confusion with the truth he brings. Regardless of what has been tradition, what has been in the past, God seeks those who worship in spirit and truth. The important issue is not where we worship or what theological stance we treasure, but whether we approach God in spirit and truth.

How astonishing that some of the deepest and most important truths of the ministry of Jesus are told to this hard-bitten, irascible woman out on a daily errand. By the Law, she is an adulterer. Her behavior and reputation have isolated her from her community. But it is to her that Jesus brings the truth.

The disciples have questions, too, but they do not ask them out loud. The text reports "they were astonished that he was speaking with a woman." Some things never change. But for the disciples, the sociological and religious taboo is so strong, they can't even voice their questions aloud. This silence, the superstition that what they see can't be spoken, is an example of a concept called "the other." The Samaritan woman is "the other." She is the other gender, the other race, and the other in her moral behavior. She is strange to the disciples, and they do not want to know anything about what is going on.

After Jesus confirms his identity as Messiah to her, the woman leaves in such a hurry to tell her neighbors that she leaves her water jar behind. She is so energized by her encounter with Christ that she cannot do anything else until she tells her story. And she witnesses with her evidence, "Come and see a man who told me everything I have ever done!" But she also witnesses with a question "Could this be the Messiah?" In her witness, the Samaritan woman doesn't have all the answers or the correct theological argument. She has her story and her question.

There are days when we are very much like the Samaritan woman. These are the times when we've just headed out to get water for the day and something has happened. We learn more of our own story, and experience in some way that Christ knows us. Sometimes that is the best witness we have. All we can say is, "This is what happened to me. What does it mean?" This is how we live the questions: we witness to one another as we share our search for faith, meaning, and truth.

The Samaritan woman's questions of Jesus kept her interacting long enough for her to experience a true faith encounter. We may get to a point of maturity or experience and come to expect that we should have more answers than questions. Or because of our place in the church others expect us to have the answers. But just when that security of being the Answer Person feels good, the questions change. In those times we have to choose whether we will be like the Samaritan woman and keep asking the questions or whether we will be silent like the disciples, scared by what is new and different into pretending that "the other" can be ignored.

This is a story for us on the days of doubt, for the days when we are overwhelmed with the trivia of our lives and wonder what is really important. It is for the days when we feel cantankerous and out of sorts. What Jesus offers us is as simple, necessary, and wonderful as a cold drink of water. The living water cleanses our spirits, makes us willing to be known, to be vulnerable again to the truth of God in our lives.

Julian of Norwich, a fourteenth-century English anchoress who lived in solitude, wrote:

> But our passing life which we have does not know in our senses what our self is, but we know in our faith. And when we know and see, truly and clearly, what our self is, then we shall truly and clearly see and know our Lord God in the fulness of love.
>
> (Paulist Press, 1978)

What are the parallels in our lives? Is it possible that our doubts come from an unwillingness to be known by God? Is it possible that a most significant part of our faith journey is becoming open to and vulnerable to being known by God? We cannot compartmentalize faith to a part of self. Acknowledging what we usually try to hide from God in dailiness or theological argument is a first step. The clarity and honesty about our whole self that we bring to communion with God is the means of worshiping in spirit and truth.

When we ask enough questions to get to the point of being known by Christ, we can truly accept, like the Samaritan woman, the gift of worshiping in spirit and in truth. We open our hands so that God's name can be written there and we can add the name "Chosen" to our own. Then we cannot help but tell our story and witness with new questions. By listening to our story, others are able to hear their own stories, find their own truth, and in Christ, ask their own questions.

The Samaritan woman asked her questions in conversation with the One who could give her living water always welling up, the One who could teach her to worship in spirit and in truth. We are not alone with our questions either. We have this communion with one another in Christ and with all those who live in our story and whose questions we share.

Sometimes it is hard to imagine that, like the Samaritan woman, our past can be redeemed—that we can be known and taught to worship in spirit and in truth. For some, it is hard to imagine that we can question cultural taboos and learn one another's truth. For others, it is hard to imagine that we don't have to do it all, the questioning, the answering, the building of the fountain and waterworks for offering living water. But we can witness by the questions we ask ourselves, one another, our community, and our nation. We have this communion in which the spirit of the Risen Christ wants to know us, and calmly waits for our questions. By our seeking, by our own quest, our lives become a living proclamation, witnesses of the living word of Jesus that we can worship in spirit and in truth, and that we can live out of the spring of water that is always welling up to nourish us.

GUIDED IMAGERY MEDITATION

Let your body settle into a comfortable position. . . . Breathe deeply and slowly.

Imagine you are walking on a dusty road. . . . The sun is hot. . . . The air is dry. . . . You have been walking all morning. . . . You are tired and thirsty. . . . Your mouth is dry and parched. . . . But you have far to go and many things to do.

A short distance away is a grove of trees. . . . As you come nearer, you hear water gurgling. . . . But as you walk faster . . . you sense a Presence with you. . . . The Spirit of Christ is here . . . waiting for you to share yourself. . . . What is the most important question in your life right now? . . . Can you ask Christ this significant question and wait for the beginning of an answer?

What part of yourself needs to be known by a loving God today? . . . Can you open yourself to Christ? . . . What truth are you willing to know about yourself? . . . Rest for a moment in the loving acceptance and joy that your willingness brings.

Go to the water. . . . Cup your hands and fill them with the cool water. . . . Drink deeply. . . . This is the inner spring . . . always welling up. . . . Claim this promise of Christ as the proclamation of your life.

Dear God,

To be known and accepted by you is one of our deepest needs. But we hide parts of ourselves from you and from others. Opening up and being vulnerable has been painful in the past and we avoid it. Grant us your assurance that when we admit all of ourselves, then we will have living water always welling up. Amen.

7

Mary of Bethany
Choosing the Better Part

Now as they went on their way, he entered a certain village, where a woman named Martha welcomed him into her home. She had a sister named Mary, who sat at the Lord's feet and listened to what he was saying. But Martha was distracted by her many tasks; so she came to him and asked, "Lord, do you not care that my sister has left me to do all the work by myself? Tell her then to help me." But the Lord answered her, "Martha, Martha, you are worried and distracted by many things; there is need of only one thing. Mary has chosen the better part, which will not be taken away from her."   **(Luke 10:38-42)**

T he greatest mother-in-law in the world used to send me the magazine *Southern Living* for a Christmas present. I looked through it regularly, clipped recipes, and sighed over the garden articles—my efforts never approached the beauty of the photos. After a few years, I found myself wondering who the people were who had time to put together all those menus, shop for the sometimes esoteric ingredients, and give those lavish parties! I just couldn't fathom who could manage all that and the rest of life, too. I finally realized I would never turn into a *Southern Living* lady. And consequently, I really identify with the conflict in this story.

Mary of Bethany's story is a familiar one. And it is one that, more than any other biblical story, poses the crucial choice between traditional roles and personal needs of women in the church today.

The story tells of an uneasy, potentially embarrassing situation for everyone. Mary leads with her heart and goes to sit at Jesus' feet. And not for a few minutes, apparently. Luke says she "stayed there listening to his words" (Luke 10:39*b* NEB). Martha's anxiety is easy to understand by anyone who has been a hostess needing help. She never stopped to consider her own needs, but went to work with cleaning and cooking to provide for her guests.

The New Revised Standard Version Bible uses the word *distracted* to convey Martha's state. And from her behavior, that must be it. She was so distracted by her anxiety over her work that she interrupted Jesus with her complaint. She doesn't appeal to Mary, but to Jesus and accuses him of not caring about the inequity her sister has created.

It's one of those situations in which the sibling rivalry of childhood has spilled over decades later. And the resentful child appeals to the parent figure to set things right. Martha, like most unquestioningly responsible siblings, has a solution to the problem: "Tell her then to help me." Is it possible that Martha in the deepest part of herself knows Mary is right, so she goes to Jesus for support?

But Jesus rebukes her gently. "Martha, Martha, you are worried and distracted by many things." And he affirms Mary's choice. She has "chosen the better part." And Jesus gives the wonderful promise: it "will not be taken away from her."

The story ends here. We are not told if Martha takes off her apron, sets aside the dish towel, and sits down to listen. We are not told of Mary's reaction. Did she feel guilty? But the conflict within us that is the root of the story goes on each day.

I believe we have trouble with the story because we cannot really believe Mary's choice is the best. All our enculturation, sometimes even within the church, is opposed to our putting our spiritual needs first.

On the first level, this story is about conflict between two people who have made different choices. But beneath that, it is about the choices all of us as women have to make every day. It is an internal conflict between the socially approved good woman caretaker and the one who feels and acts on the God-given right to take time and energy for her own spiritual nurturance. In our overscheduled and busy culture, the decision to attend to our spiritual needs may cause others to actually or obliquely term our withdrawal selfish. We may judge ourselves so, too.

Carol Gilligan has written a book, *In a Different Voice*, in which she analyzes the unconscious rule that women raised in our society must be not just unselfish, but often selfless to be considered "good, ethical, and moral." To devote time, energy, and money to personal development and goals is called selfish and is inherently bad; to devote all our lives to others as the caricature of the perfect mother is the only way to be considered a moral person.

Martha is selfless to this point, caretaking until she is resentful. Her selflessness is harmful to her and to her relationship with her sister. A large part of the problem is our unspoken expectations. If we have *Southern Living* expectations that imperfect food or entertaining is unworthy of our guests, we will often be overwhelmed and resentful.

Another way to look at this conflict is the difference between "task" and "process" orientation. Most of us grow up to tend toward one or the other in our approach to setting priorities and problem solving. But both have their uses, and we need to learn the tools of each and develop the ability to use whichever one is required.

Martha's absolute task orientation is what Jesus rebukes. She is literally busy with too many things. Especially for women who are overwhelmed, what Mary does is choose the better part—the time for a personal relationship with Christ, which develops in time spent apart in study and communion. It is this kind of time that nourishes us and allows us to learn from the deepest part of ourselves what limits to put on the "many things" that the world brings to us.

That list can grow longer with each morning newspaper for the conscientious woman—the poor and homeless, AIDS victims, the environment, human rights, and hunger. Martha's task orientation would lead her to create a committee for each issue that came in her mailbox. Mary has learned the process orientation of nature; she can seek the leading of Christ, depend on it, and grow from it.

Lest we continue to assume this dichotomy, we must remember that it is a false dichotomy. We are all Martha and Mary and need to express both caretaking and contemplating. The historical primary assumption of contemplation, study, and proclamation by men has left women with the caretaking as their apparent only choice by default. Yearning to sit with Christ and learn, we are vexed by all the work that needs doing in every arena of our lives.

The process of nature can inform us of the way we can meet these needs. Think of how slowly the seasons change. Think of the life cycle of a plant. Our spiritual development requires some discipline, but we cannot decide on a goal of being a more spiritual person and devise a list of simple jots and tittles that will make this happen. We must consider the lilies of the field. We must be still and know. We must withdraw to a quiet place and wait on the Lord.

GUIDED IMAGERY MEDITATION

Take a deep breath . . . and another. . . . It is a busy holiday. . . . You are visiting a family member . . . the house is full of people. . . . Other women in the family are busy in the kitchen. . . . Good smells waft through the house. . . .

Feeling a need for solitude, you search out a quiet corner . . . and look out a window. . . . Outside something draws your attention. . . . Near the ground . . . a few green leaves of a spring bulb have come through the ground. . . . Think of the bulb, resting in the dark earth. . . . It absorbs moisture and nutrients that are provided for it. . . . So slowly that you cannot see, the leaves will grow, then the flower will come up to bloom in the sun. . . . Let this peaceful promise settle deep inside. . . .

Then an anxious voice breaks through. . . . "Would you come lend a hand in the kitchen?" she asks. . . .

What is your reaction? . . .

What one thing is necessary? . . .

Look back out the window . . . What grace do you need from this quiet time?

Listen as the promise comes. . . . "This shall not be taken away from you." . . .

Dear God,

We confess our busyness, Lord. We confess our fussing and fretting about many things that distract us from what is necessary.

Comfort our Martha side, dear God. Grant us time and the reminder that we can choose the best part. Fill our hearts with the affirmation that when we make time for communion with thee, the joy of that time shall not be taken away. Amen.

8

The Bent-over Woman
What Needs Healing?

And just then there appeared a woman with a spirit that had crippled her for eighteen years. She was bent over and was quite unable to stand up straight. When Jesus saw her, he called her over and said, "Woman, you are set free from your ailment." When he laid his hands on her, immediately she stood up straight and began praising God. But the leader of the synagogue, indignant because Jesus had cured on the sabbath, kept saying to the crowd, "There are six days on which work ought to be done; come on those days and be cured, and not on the sabbath day." But the Lord answered him and said, "You hypocrites! Does not each of you on the sabbath untie his ox or his donkey from the manger, and lead it away to give it water? And ought not this woman, a daughter of Abraham whom Satan bound for eighteen long years, be set free from this bondage on the sabbath day?" When he said this, all his opponents were put to shame; and the entire crowd was rejoicing at all the wonderful things that he was doing.   **(Luke 13:11-17)**

T hough she lives in my neighborhood and waits on the corner regularly for the city bus, I don't know her name. She is a dignified, older woman who dresses carefully. She always has on a hat and gloves, her coat is brushed, and in winter, she wears heavy white stockings. She is bent over. Her back is curved forward at a severe angle. Her head and face look out at a limited world. I doubt she can see over the tops of cars that go by. How long has it been since she has seen clouds or stars?

She makes me remember other bent-over women I have known. One was a young mother in a parent education program in a rural school. Content with no running water and an outhouse, she longed only to take her children to see exotic animals in a city zoo. Years of demeaning poverty had led her to a life dream of just one such trip.

One bright woman works at a fast food restaurant. It is the only job she can get to support her baby daughter, since the father has long since moved out of state.

Another young mother mutilates her body with razor blades when she recovers new memories of her father's sexual abuse. The physical pain is easier to bear than the shame and terror.

And there are the women in a large company who suffer sexual harassment and discrimination on a regular basis. They have just given up the fight.

All these women have something in common with the bent-over woman. They are bent over by burdens so old, the limited vision they have seems like the only world they are allowed. Like the bent-over woman, they need a healing touch.

The story of the bent-over woman is a wonderful and powerful story. The woman is anonymous; like many of the women of the Bible, she is not named. But the healing she receives and the place and time in which it takes place are very significant for women in the church today.

The story and parable preceding this story in chapter 13 set the stage for interpretation. The story is a virtually unknown one about Pilate mixing the blood of Galileans with pagan sacrifices. Jesus very clearly states that such suffering is no indication of greater sin. Or what about those victims who were killed in a freak accident by a falling tower in verse 4? They were no worse offenders than all sinners.

The parable concerns a fig tree that had not borne fruit for three years. The owner wanted to cut it down, but the gardener asked for one more year in which to till and feed the tree—to give it one more chance to bear fruit.

In Jesus' day, the common belief about physical or mental suffering was that it was caused by possession of an evil spirit. And this possession occurred because the victim was morally or spiritually deficient in some way. Some people still operate on this belief and go to public religious charlatans who promise healing for illnesses these people attribute to their sins.

But Jesus, by relating the story and parable, is declaring that physical suffering cannot simply be judged as evidence of moral or spiritual shortcoming. When one's life does not bear "fruit," a person is in need of a gardener who knows how to feed and nurture the potential inside that person.

The bent-over woman does not seek Jesus out. She has come to the synagogue on the Sabbath, we may assume, as has been her habit during the eighteen years of an affliction that has so crippled her spine she cannot stand straight at all. For eighteen years, she has seen only the ground, no sky or clouds or stars.

Jesus calls her to him and heals her in the synagogue on the Sabbath. Notice the words that convey the healing: "You are set free from your ailment." With a straight back, she stands up to praise God.

Then the story broadens to show the reactions of religious leaders to Jesus' healing on the Sabbath. Healing for one individual has social ramifications. The leader of the synagogue is irate. This kind of work is not to be done on the Sabbath. The bent-over woman is humble and apparently followed the rules and remained bent over for eighteen years.

Notice that the words of the church leader are not directed to Jesus, the person who has actually angered and threatened him. Instead, he "triangles the conflict," by speaking to a third party—the people who are watching. Jesus has once again shown the religious "system" to be one that is not sensitive to people's suffering. The only recourse for the synagogue leader is to fall back on the traditional, but unexamined rules. He wants to remind the people of the Law.

By synagogue "rules," healing is "work." It is the "work" of the synagogue and its officials. So by Sabbath law, no one should expect to be cured on the Sabbath. In this system, healing is not part of God's grace, but the works righteousness of the religious system and its leaders. Since he sees healing as within the power of the system he serves, the synagogue leader can limit the days on which healing is possible.

Demonstrating their hypocrisy, Jesus points out that they all had taken care of their oxen or donkeys on the Sabbath by letting them out of the manger to drink. This argument points out two significant parts to the hypocrisy. First, doing the work of caring for a donkey or oxen was a matter of economic survival. Thus the religious leaders made allowances for such "work." If the people could not maintain their own economic survival, neither could the synagogue. So the exception was one related to the self-interest of the religious leaders.

Second, Jesus' example is full of irony when we realize that women's status in that culture was not much higher than beasts of burden. Both were considered property of men to be provided for or set aside (or cut down like the fig tree) as the owner decided.

Jesus is making the point here that his healing makes a distinction between the suffering of human beings and the care provided to animals as economic survival. How much more important that a woman crippled for eighteen years should be healed and freed to stand straight and praise God!

Many women today inside and outside the church are bent over: crippled by physical, emotional, or spiritual affliction. Too many women do not live out their lives standing straight up and looking without fear into the future. The kinds and causes of "bent-overness" are many. They include physical and sexual violence, depression, poverty, lack of education, and economic and political discrimination.

And any affliction that has been long-term can lead to the state of hopelessness. How do we see past what has bent us down for years?

The bent-over woman was healed because she was faithful. She had been coming, perhaps with fainter and fainter hope all those eighteen years. For her, and for us, sometimes the most significant healing comes when we least expect it and from people who surprise us with their compassion. The power of God's healing, the lifting of our burdens, stands ready. We have to be ready for the changes that such healing brings. The story of the bent-over woman promises that there is healing available beyond religious practice and our own expectations.

Imagine how her life had changed. For eighteen years, she had been looking at the ground, dependent on sounds and intuitions about what the world was like and about her place in it. The same is true for any kind of crippling. Life lived in a diminished state for a long period of time distorts our perceptions of the world and our place in it.

Just as the bent-over woman had a whole new perception of

the world and herself after her healing, so also we may find that our world view and our self-concept change when we experience the power of God's free grace. It is also possible that the people with religious or political status will be threatened by our new view. Like the bent-over woman, we can hear Jesus say, "Ought not this woman be set free from this bondage?"

GUIDED IMAGERY MEDITATION

Find a comfortable, alert posture. . . . Close your eyes and take a few, deep, slow breaths.

It is a Sunday morning. . . . You are walking down a sidewalk toward your church. . . . As you walk, think of a burden that bows you down. . . . You have felt this burden for a long time . . . for years. . . . Your affliction has become so heavy and oppressive that your head is bent down. . . . Your shoulders are curved in and down from this burden. . . . You can see only the gray concrete as you come to the church door.

A voice calls to you. . . . Your burden is so heavy you cannot lift your head, but only turn toward the voice. . . . Then you feel gentle hands on your back and the voice says. . . . "You are rid of your burden. . . . Your affliction is gone . . . You are set free."

You feel warmth and strength in your back and shoulders. . . . Slowly you straighten. . . . The words are true. . . . Your affliction is gone.

When you stand, you see the faces of others who recognize the change in you. . . . How do you react? . . . What is the praise you speak in their hearing?

Dear God,

As women busy with careers, children, and church work, it is easy to identify with the bent-over woman. Often we feel burdened, bent over with cares.

If the church seems to be saying "Come another day for healing," it is nearly impossible to imagine and hope for healing and the lifting of our burdens. Grant us new minds and hearts open to the hope of your blessed healing. Remind us to stand straight and praise you when it happens. Amen.

9

The Woman Taken in Adultery
Blessing and Forgiveness

Early in the morning he came again to the temple. All the people came to him and he sat down and began to teach them. The scribes and the Pharisees brought a woman who had been caught in adultery; and making her stand before all of them, they said to him, "Teacher, this woman was caught in the very act of committing adultery. Now in the law Moses commanded us to stone such women. Now what do you say?" They said this to test him, so that they might have some charge to bring against him. Jesus bent down and wrote with his finger on the ground. When they kept on questioning him, he straightened up and said to them, "Let anyone among you who is without sin be the first to throw a stone at her." And once again he bent down and wrote on the ground. When they heard it, they went away, one by one, beginning with the elders; and Jesus was left alone with the woman standing before him. Jesus straightened up and said to her, "Woman, where are they? Has no one condemned you?" She said, "No one, sir." And Jesus said, "Neither do I condemn you. Go your way, and from now on do not sin again."   **(John 8:2-11)**

My friend was anguished over her awareness that she simply could not take a walk by herself after dark in her city neighborhood. One night, that was her clear desire and need. But she did not feel safe; in spite of the fact that it was a residential neighborhood, the statistics of sexual assault against women in her city were against her. She stayed inside, trapped and unhappy.

Another friend stepped outside to watch the stars while visiting her mother in a university town. She reports the overwhelming sadness and tears when she realized that she did not feel safe in her own city to do the same because there is a bar just a short distance away from her home in another residential area. Different stories, the same fear.

Women still have to be careful in our day. To be certain they are safe and free from any public question of their motivation, women lead restricted lives. Publicly, our bodies and our sexuality do not belong to us, but to the world's interpretation of our behavior, dress, and speech.

Rape and sexual assault, sexual abuse and harassment, abortion: the media, courts, and legislatures are full of public debate about what are seen as negative consequences of women's sexuality. In spite of decades of work by activists, lawyers, and judges, a woman accusing a man of rape is still often subjected to a humiliating public ordeal, with her own behavior suspect and vulnerable to accusation. Perpetrators of sexual abuse against minors are seldom reported, much less prosecuted. Women in the workplace report sexual harassment as a common problem. And when women assert the right to privacy on the issue of abortion, the subject becomes the most divisive public moral argument of our time.

The story of the woman caught in adultery is one in which the private becomes public. And women today are only too aware that what should be private—their own possession of their bodies and ownership of their sexuality—is still too often a matter of public determination.

And often it is for the same reasons as this woman in John's Gospel. Her private behavior, her private sin, is used as a public test: Will the religious power of the tradition silence this new upstart Messiah? The woman herself, as a human being, is irrelevant to the purpose of the scribes and Pharisees. Her body, her sexuality, are only tools in their plan to bring a charge against Jesus.

Jesus is in the Temple. He is in their place. And he is teaching the people. He is, without their permission or their acceptance, doing what the Pharisees consider their purview. This simple act, sitting in the Temple teaching the people, threatens the whole structure of Judaic tradition. Jesus is not a rabbi who has been brought along in the system. He has not, in the eyes of the leaders, earned the religious right to sit in the Temple and teach. This alone is an abomination to them. That he would claim direct revelation from God, speak to the people of that revelation, and be called Messiah violated the entire history of religious law and the structures that supported the Pharisees' work.

So they need a dramatic, public event to challenge this preacher from Galilee. Surely, even this radical from the country would not countermand Mosaic law; that would make him suspect even in the eyes of the people who listen to him. By making the case public, the leaders hope to put Jesus in a no-win situation. Either he would capitulate to the Law or be at risk of the people's condemnation.

Somehow, the Pharisees and scribes find their test case. The woman is unnamed, but her private act has become public and her life is at risk. The real intent of the Pharisees can be seen in the person who is missing from this scene. Where is her partner? If she was caught in the act, there was a man there somewhere. But in their haste to discredit Jesus, the religious leaders do not apply the Levitical law as it is written. The reference in Leviticus 20:10 says that both the man and the woman involved in adultery shall be put to death. So, in selecting only the woman and never mentioning the man, the Pharisees and scribes have selectively applied the Law that they attempt to use against Jesus. This reveals a lack of respect for the whole Law among those who publicly proclaim themselves as the upholders of the Law.

As Jesus does so often, he transforms the situation that is set to trap him and confounds those who challenge his word and ministry. First, he is silent and bends down to write in the dirt. This action has confused interpreters for years. Was Jesus biding his time, waiting on inspiration? The Pharisees press the question. And Jesus stands back up with his response, which shames and silences the religious leaders. The rigid and absolutized Mosaic law is to be transformed by one based on personal responsibility. Vehement public righteousness must be measured against the darkness of one's own heart.

Jesus preaches a sermon in a sentence, and the Pharisees and scribes fail his test. Challenged to stone the woman based on their own judgment of themselves, the leaders know they cannot act. And they quietly leave the scene.

Jesus' statement accomplishes another change in how the law

about private sin is to be applied. The Pharisees and scribes have picked the sin of adultery, one which would be seen as preeminent in the people's eyes. This is still the situation today; too often we concentrate not only on others' sin instead of our own, but we are also quickest to condemn sexual sin above all others. Just as there must have been jeers by the crowd in the Temple, so also are we titillated by news of sexual sin. But Jesus levels the hierarchy of sin. Sin, regardless of whether it is public or private, sexual or nonsexual, is still sin and all sin is equal in the eyes of God.

The religious leaders have left, but the woman and the palpable tension in this scene remain. She has remained standing during all this time. What must she have been thinking? Humiliated or defiant, she has been turned over to this strange teacher by those who held power over her. And this quiet man's posture and manner is not haughty and domineering like the others. What is he doing here, kneeling before her and writing on the ground? What kind of man places himself physically below a woman publicly accused of adultery?

Then Jesus straightens up and speaks directly to the woman for the first time. His question marks the true judgment for this woman. She has been accused of adultery. But whatever the evidence or witnesses that the religious leaders had, it is not enough to condemn her. The entire public case was a sham. There is no one to condemn her. She speaks her only words in this story, "No one, sir," and states her personal truth. Whatever she has done, there is no one to condemn her now.

And this strange, gentle man releases her from the public humiliation, from the trauma of the morning's frightening events. "Neither do I condemn you. Go your way and from now on do not sin again." Jesus does not ask for confession from this woman; he makes no attempt to establish guilt or innocence about her behavior. Her private sexual behavior is her own business. If she is guilty, she has been forgiven. And forgiveness makes her sexuality her own responsibility again; she should sin no more.

This story presents the same challenge to us today as it did to the people watching the scene. The issues of the day call for our words as women about ourselves as women, including our sexuality. But the church does not often help us to do this. The church is divided over abortion; it is too often silent about rape, sexual assault, and sexual abuse, and is ambivalent about sexual harassment. And too often the tradition manages to convey that women's speech about women's sexuality is the equivalent of religious adultery. That is, when we speak publicly about these issues, we have violated the unspoken, but sacrosanct "law" to be silent above all about issues related to our sexuality.

Brennan Manning has said that as humans we often bargain with God by saying, "Lord, if I change, you'll love me, won't you?" The Lord's reply is always, "You don't have to change so I'll love you; I love you so you'll change." This is the message of Jesus to the woman accused of adultery and to all of us. Whether we are the one accused or those standing with stones at the ready, the wisdom of Jesus can transform our way of thinking about sexuality and we can become responsible for ourselves and our behavior.

GUIDED IMAGERY MEDITATION

Find a comfortable, yet alert posture for your body. . . . Begin breathing deeply and slowly. . . . Pay attention to your body. . . . Where there is muscle tension . . . let go.

Your body is a glorious gift of God . . . but the world . . . or important people in it . . . may not have recognized that. . . . Remember a time when you were shamed because of your body. . . . Or when you were afraid . . . because of your body.

Where were you? . . . Remember the scene . . . Who laid undeserved shame on you?

Now imagine the presence of Jesus in the scene. . . . His demeanor is quiet and calm. . . . When the shaming words are said, . . . he speaks firmly and clearly. . . . What do you hear? . . . At his words, your accuser leaves.

Now Jesus looks at you. . . . His eyes are warm and kind, full of mercy. . . . He says, "No one condemns you. Neither do I. . . . Go your way and be whole."

Feel yourself open to receive his merciful words. . . . Take them deeply into your soul. . . . Rest in this assurance.

Dear God,

Sometimes we cannot discern the difference in the world's judgment of us as women and who we know ourselves to be in your eyes. Sometimes we are caught in the whirlwind of self-condemnation and it is hard to accept your words of love and forgiveness.

We confess that because we have been judged falsely, we often judge others too quickly. Teach us wisdom to know ourselves, to separate false shame and guilt from what is our responsibility. Free us that we may be able to live in the power of your grace, which redeems and transforms us. Amen.

Sisters of Faith

10

Hannah
Making a Sacrifice

On the day when Elkanah sacrificed, he would give portions to his wife Peninnah and to all her sons and daughters; but to Hannah he gave a double portion, because he loved her, though the LORD had closed her womb. Her rival used to provoke her severely, to irritate her, because the LORD had closed her womb. So it went on year by year; as often as she went up to the house of the LORD, she used to provoke her. Therefore Hannah wept and would not eat.

She was deeply distressed and prayed to the LORD, and wept bitterly. She made this vow: "O LORD of hosts, if only you will look on the misery of your servant, and remember me, and not forget your servant, but will give to your servant a male child, then I will set him before you as a nazirite until the day of his death. He shall drink neither wine nor intoxicants, and no razor shall touch his head."

As she continued praying before the LORD, Eli observed her mouth. Hannah was praying silently; only her lips moved, but her voice was not heard; therefore Eli thought she was drunk. So Eli said to her, "How long will you make a drunken spectacle of yourself? Put away your wine." But Hannah answered, "No, my lord, I am a woman deeply troubled; I have drunk neither wine nor strong drink, but I have been pouring out my soul before the LORD. Do not regard your servant as a worthless woman, for I have been speaking out of my great anxiety and vexation all this time." Then Eli answered, "Go in peace; the God of Israel grant the petition you have made to him." And she said, "Let your servant find favor in your sight." Then the woman went to her quarters, ate and drank with her husband, and her countenance was sad no longer.

They rose early in the morning and worshiped before the LORD; then they went back to their house at Ramah. Elkanah knew his wife Hannah, and the LORD remembered her. In due time Hannah conceived and bore a son. She named him Samuel, for she said, "I have asked him of the LORD."

And she said, "Oh, my lord! As you live, my lord, I am the woman who was standing here in your presence, praying to the LORD. For this child I prayed; and the LORD has granted me the petition that I made to him. Therefore I have lent him to the LORD; as long as he lives, he is given to the LORD."

She left him there for the LORD.

(1 Samuel 1:4-7, 10-20, 26-28)

Parked a few blocks from work, I sat in my locked car and cried. The dream job had deteriorated into power struggles and overwhelming demands on my ability to care for needy individuals. It was time to make a change, admit I was not Supermom and could not handle a full-time job, be the mother and wife I wanted to be, and stay involved in my church.

You have seen the magazine articles and commercials. They offer a part of the story of contemporary American women, and thus create a myth. The limitations and personal costs of trying to be Supermom are not often discussed. Instead, the lists of obligations to job, family, and community often become almost unconscious sacrifices of the personal individuality of self, which is a gift from God. Underneath the multiplicity of roles, who are we and what do we want to offer to God?

In times of stress, the word *sacrifice* takes on a negative connotation. We have lost the original meaning, which is an offering to be made sacred by God. In the Old Testament, it was an act of consecration, not one of self-denial.

Too often, we reserve consideration of the sacred to Sunday mornings and holy days of the church calendar. This makes it easy to assume that it is our giving that is sacrificial. But whether our offering of lives, time, and money is made sacred or not is up to God. Since our other days seem so full of self-sacrifice, whether freely chosen or not, even the word may seem threatening.

Hannah's sacrifice seems so radical—leaving a three-year-old boy with a strange priest. How can she do this? For herself, she is giving up the hours and days of watching him grow. But a reexamination of the whole story may bring a different picture than the one we remember from Sunday school. There Hannah is in the background holding a new robe, but she is not in the background in the biblical account.

Hannah's barrenness, like Sarah's, is a personal and social burden. She experiences the same taunting from a rival in her husband's household. And she is humiliated each time a sacrifice is offered. What should be days of worship and celebration are just depressing reminders for Hannah. Her story is the story of all women who desperately want children, and who wait, year after year, with empty arms.

Elkanah tries to comfort her with his love, but Hannah will seek the Lord. Her pleas are the appeals of the psalms of lament. They reveal her humility: "If only you will look on the misery of your servant, and remember me." Hannah's sacrifice is that of a broken spirit. Her vow is the offering of a son to God's purpose.

She is so fervent that Eli mistakenly believes that she is drunk. Hannah is so certain of her purposes that she assertively defends herself to Eli. What appears to be strange public behavior is actually the "pouring out of her soul." It is such a poignant phrase; she is in anguish and her only resource is prayer. Eli is convinced and gives her a blessing.

Hannah seeks God's intervention in her life situation. She initiates the sacred aspect of sacrifice by making her greatest desire an offering. Her sacrifice is not a ritual one based in the law, but one of a humble heart. And she is empowered by her offering.

Her husband Elkanah recognizes it when he accedes to her decision about weaning the child before taking him to Eli. This marriage is not a typically patriarchal one. Elkanah respects the vow made in prayer by his wife, and her interpretation of how it is to be carried out.

Hannah is one of three women in the Bible who has a psalm recorded. She praises God's salvation, holiness, and power, and acknowledges God's blessing for all who have been humiliated. Her song is a precursor to the Magnificat of Mary in Luke 1, as well as being prophetic: she mentions a future king though Israel is still ruled by judges. It will be Samuel's role to anoint Saul, the first king of Israel.

Hannah does not go unrewarded. Eli pronounces a blessing

when Samuel is brought to the temple and later Hannah is given three sons and two daughters.

We have misunderstood God's true expectation of our sacrifice. It is not to exhaust ourselves, mentally and physically meeting the demands of the roles we fill. It does not mean being totally unselfish in the face of loved ones' needs until we are filled with resentment. Such resentment grows if we cannot say "No." When our days are filled with "oughts" imposed by others, we no longer have the time or energy to "offer" ourselves to God and be made sacred.

When we are overwhelmed, we are often suffused with feelings of guilt and envy, even though our heads echo righteous sentences. Too many unconscious sacrifices prevent us from seeking God's power in conscious sacrifice. What can we offer to God in the possibility of being made sacred by God?

Hannah prayed for what she was willing to give up. Giving up, letting go, offering up are ways of experiencing the power of freedom before God. The first necessity is to examine our roles, tasks, and expectations in order to discover whether there is anything left to make as a conscious, deliberate offering to God. We, too, can be empowered to live by our intentional sacrifices and thus to experience once again singing praise to God.

GUIDED IMAGERY MEDITATION

Find a relaxed, yet alert position. Close your eyes and breathe deeply . . . and again.

You are standing in a room. . . . There are tall windows in the room. . . . Sunlight is streaming in. . . . A light breeze blows through the room. . . . The air is clear. . . . The sunlight is warm.

In the center of the room is a large table and a single chair. . . . Sit down in the chair . . . and look at the objects on the table.

There is a set of car keys . . . Do you need to change your focus of service and go somewhere to those in need?

There is a photograph album of family and friends. . . . Do you need to give up some of your caretaking to risk something new for God?

There is a clock . . . Do you need to give God more of your time for quiet communion?

Consider the symbols. . . . What do you want to offer to God? . . . Pick up the object. . . . Hold it gently in your open hands. . . . Raise your hands and offer your sacrifice to God. . . . Freely you have received. . . . Freely give.

Dear God,

Sacrifice is a hard word. We confess that we do not think much about it today. Help us to remember that what is important to you is that we make our sacrifice consciously and deliberately. Be with us to guide and support us as we renew our offerings to you. May we be like Hannah and freely give in gratitude for your love and in celebration of your glory. Amen.

11

Martha
Faith Beyond Grief

When Jesus arrived, he found that Lazarus had already been in the tomb four days. Now Bethany was near Jerusalem, some two miles away, and many of the Jews had come to Martha and Mary to console them about their brother. When Martha heard that Jesus was coming, she went and met him, while Mary stayed at home. Martha said to Jesus, "Lord, if you had been here, my brother would not have died. But even now I know that God will give you whatever you ask of him." Jesus said to her, "Your brother will rise again." Martha said to him, "I know that he will rise again in the resurrection on the last day." Jesus said to her, "I am the resurrection and the life. Those who believe in me, even though they die, will live, and everyone who lives and believes in me will never die. Do you believe this?" She said to him, "Yes, Lord, I believe that you are the Messiah, the Son of God, the one coming into the world."   **(John 11:17-27)**

My office for Women in Ministry was over the kitchen at church. Our kitchen manager brought her young son while she prepared the Wednesday supper. Sam was patient for a while, then I heard him: "I want to go home. I want to go home now." But it was wonderful to hear his voice because Sam came into this world almost three months too early, and his parents, sister, and our whole church waited for God to work a miracle that summer.

My husband's phone call came while I was out of town. His news sent a chill over me. For the third time, this couple's baby had come much too early. The first two had not survived, and we did not know whether to dare to hope. I had started a baby afghan and decided that the only way I could deal with the fear was to make the crochet stitches a matter of prayer for Sam and his family. How could they possibly survive more grief? How could faith live beyond so much heartache?

The word for Martha is *faithful*. And most churches depend on the "Marthas" of the faith to get the daily work of the church done. Their faith is a stalwart one, learned through the days and years of opening their hearts and hands to what God would have them do.

When Martha's name is mentioned, the first story most of us think of is probably the one in which she rebukes her sister Mary for not helping around the house when guests are expected. Martha doesn't come off too well. In that story her faith has turned into obsession about how a perfect hostess would provide for her guests. She sounds bitter and exhausted, and even Jesus admonishes her. Martha's work is important, but too often invisible, and her spirit in Luke's story is not one most women would want to emulate. Perhaps Martha has a faith that goes beyond the tasks her housekeeping requires.

The story in John adds another, larger dimension, and perhaps one that puts Martha's faithfulness in caretaking in a spiritual context. This is the story of the raising of Lazarus from the dead, and the reactions of his sisters to Jesus' belated arrival. Martha goes out to meet Jesus, and in verses 21 through 27 makes several statements of undaunted faith.

Initially, Martha's first statement asserting that the presence of Jesus would have prevented Lazarus' death could be interpreted as either confrontation or a simple statement of faith. In a state of grief, even for those who are used to being strong and in charge, there can be anger at others who bear responsibility and relationship. This comes out of one stage of denial in the grief process. It is a cry that somehow, someone could have changed the terrible reality.

Martha's next statement is also enigmatic. Is she simply stating a belief in the power of Jesus to command God's intervention in a crisis? Or is the statement a desperate bargain, even a manipulation?

Martha's faith is not a simplistic one. She could not be a Pollyanna who blithely maintains a public faith to hide from her inner doubts. Martha's faith is one that grows out of a test that has two parts. The first part is the death of her brother and the delay in Jesus' arrival. This is the inevitable anguished question: Why didn't he come when they notified him? How could such a death and the sisters' grief be reconciled with the message of their friend, Jesus, the Messiah? All those strangers had been healed or saved by Jesus. Why not Lazarus, one of his beloved friends? What possible faith meaning can this terrible reality have?

The first part of Martha's test of faith is not spoken directly. She does not ask her questions aloud. But the second part is direct and comes in the form of Jesus' responses to Martha. First he makes a clear promise: "Your brother will rise again." Like the disciples, Martha misinterprets this promise. In her grief, she cannot believe that this promise is to be fulfilled in the present time. Surely Jesus means in the future, "in the resurrection on the last day."

Then Jesus makes the statement of his identity and his purpose: "I am the resurrection and the life. Those who believe in me, even though they die, will live." Martha and Lazarus do not have to wait for the future, for the last day. New life is possible now, in this present moment.

But Martha must commit. She must answer the direct question: "Do you believe this?" New life and faith are part and parcel of each other. And Martha's answer is clear and affirming: "I believe that you are the Messiah, the Son of God, the one coming into the world."

Martha's faith calls her beyond her everyday tasks and her deep grief to a witness that is unwavering. She believes and is unequivocal.

Martha is a hard example to follow. She makes a very strong statement of faith at a time of great loss in her life. Death is the last complete mystery to us. Shelves of books on religion and philosophy have been written about the human fear of death. It is a great paradox to engage the idea in Martha's story that loss and faith are intertwined. Times of great grief and loss in our lives make us ask the hard questions of God. Why? Why this loss and this unbearable pain?

Perhaps it is the geography of Martha's story that gives us a hint of how Martha arrived at her strong faith statement. For

Martha does not stay home this time, busy as a hostess for the funeral guests. She leaves and goes out to meet Jesus on the road, to confront him with the reality of her brother's death. Her first step to faith is the literal first step out of the house of grief and loss.

Renewal of faith beyond grief or loss is not a matter of simple words about God's will. A loving God does not will death and loss. Faith in new life comes out of and beyond a struggle of questions, anguish, and confrontation. Do we believe in life after death? Do we believe in life in the midst of death? Do we have faith in the renewal of joy in our lives in spite of depression and despair?

Martha's faith was not a simple one. She came to it out of her seeking. Our faith today, in a world filled with human trauma, cannot be a simple one either. In prayer and worship, we bring our suffering, our losses, our confusions, and our sense of overwhelming responsibility to God.

GUIDED IMAGERY MEDITATION

Sit quietly. Take a few slow, deep breaths. . . . Relax and let go of the daily duties that are pressing in right now. . . . Let go.

Imagine you are sitting in a room. . . . The room is associated with a sense of loss or grief that you have in your life right now. . . . Imagine the details of the room . . . the color . . . the walls . . . the furniture. . . . Picture a symbol of your loss in the room and look at it. . . . What are the particular things you miss?

Now imagine that you are getting up and walking to a door in the room. . . . The door leads outside and you walk through. . . . Outside the light is bright. . . . There is a road in front of the house. . . . Walk down the road.

Soon you sense the presence of Jesus. . . . What question would you ask Jesus? . . . Tell him what you need to say. . . . Listen for a response. . . . Jesus has a question for you. . . . What is it? . . . How do you respond? . . . Hold on to the assurance of faith that you find.

Dear God,

Faith is sometimes so hard. We don't understand why faith comes and goes. Grant us courage, God, to step out of rooms full of grief and self-pity and doubt. Help us to sense your presence as we step out in hope of renewed faith and toward new challenges that faith brings. Amen.

12

Mary Magdalene
Called to Proclaim

Then the disciples returned to their homes. But Mary stood weeping outside the tomb. As she wept, she bent over to look into the tomb; and she saw two angels in white, sitting where the body of Jesus had been lying, one at the head and the other at the feet. They said to her, "Woman, why are you weeping?" She said to them, "They have taken away my Lord, and I do not know where they have laid him." When she had said this, she turned around and saw Jesus standing there, but she did not know that it was Jesus. Jesus said to her, "Woman, why are you weeping? Whom are you looking for?" Supposing him to be the gardener, she said to him, "Sir, if you have carried him away, tell me where you have laid him, and I will take him away." Jesus said to her, "Mary!" She turned and said to him in Hebrew, "Rabbouni!" (which means Teacher). Jesus said to her, "Do not hold on to me, because I have not yet ascended to the Father. But go to my brothers and say to them, 'I am ascending to my Father and your Father, to my God and your God.'" Mary Magdalene went and announced to the disciples, "I have seen the Lord"; and she told them that he had said these things to her.

(John 20:10-18)

Most of us have at least one demon. Most of us feel at times that there is a part of our personality or spiritual identity that is both unwholesome and impervious to change. Jungian therapists call this our "dark side." Ironically enough, the dark side is often an exaggeration of a positive quality; for example, pride is more self-confidence and self-reliance than anyone is justified in feeling.

The one identifying statement about Mary Magdalene in any of the Gospels is that she was a woman from whom Jesus had cast out seven demons (Mark 16:9). Sometimes the text gives a hint of what effect the demon had on the victim. But we are given no hint of that about Mary Magdalene. What could have been the seven demons? What could this stand for in her story?

We can only speculate. Demons usually stood for either physical or mental illness. "Possessed by a demon" was the primitive way of explaining terrible human pain and bizarre behavior. Common belief held that evil spirits were alive and unseen and could inhabit human beings. This belief could be used to explain immoral or aberrant social behavior. Being demon-possessed was a way to explain someone who didn't fit in with normal society, perhaps one who challenged accepted mores.

Seven different demons would imply that Mary Magdalene experienced extreme personal suffering. Strangely enough, the story of her healing is left out. The only evidence we have is her behavior after the healing.

Mary Magdalene is the only woman mentioned in all four Gospels as being present at both the crucifixion and the tomb. In spite of this prominence, she is a shadowy figure in New Testament interpretation.

The picture we have been given of Mary Magdalene through both academic and popular interpretation is a distorted one. She is sometimes considered to be the sinful woman who anoints Jesus' feet in chapter 7 of Luke. And, of course, to many traditional interpreters, "sinful woman" means only one thing—prostitution. So in the script for *The Last Temptation of Christ*, she is portrayed as a prostitute. In *Jesus Christ Superstar*, the same identification is made. Probably it is this association that made both the early church, and writers and preachers of our day reluctant to use Magdalene's faith and witness as examples to women in the church.

But there is no biblical basis for this identification of Mary Magdalene. Her name is mentioned in the book of Luke in the chapter immediately following the story of the anointing woman. That narrative closeness is the only possible reason to associate Mary with the "sinful woman."

She was not completely without resources. According to Luke 8, she was one of the women who followed Jesus and "provided for them out of their resources." The women were funding this traveling band and their leader.

There is no family mentioned for this Mary, though there is for every other Mary in the New Testament. In fact, most of them are identified by their relationships—sister of Martha, mother of James, mother of Jesus. By implication, Mary of Magdalene is one who has heeded the injunction of Jesus to leave the security of human family and join with the family of faith.

The incidence of her name in Gospel accounts leaves a primary impression that Mary Magdalene was a significant woman among the followers of Jesus. Her prominence would not have been based merely in her financial means. Jesus had healed her of suffering, and most likely had relieved her of public ridicule as well. He had redeemed a life that would have been condemned by ignorance. Whatever the seven demons represented, she was free of them because of Jesus. She was free to be her own person and she chose to follow this itinerant rabbi. She acted out her healing by a devotion unique in the Gospels.

Her devotion leads her to his cross. She does not have the power over his life that he had over hers. She cannot save him. All she can do is be present nearby on the day of his crucifixion. And after the crucifixion, she honors his death by her plan to anoint his body, her vigil at the tomb, and her tears. Then after the Sabbath, Mary Magdalene returns.

According to John, she first comes by herself "while it was still dark." When she discovers the stone rolled away, she runs to get Peter and John. They hurry to investigate, and John hesitates at the entrance. Then Peter goes in, and John follows. The evidence of the empty tomb and linen wrappings is confusing to them: "they did not understand the scripture." So the two men turn around and go home.

But Mary Magdalene stays. She weeps, overcome by grief that the body of her redeemer was gone. She has come in a final act of devotion to anoint him with spices. Now that was not possible.

She looks once more, and this time the tomb is not empty. There are two angels there who ask a simple question, "Why are you weeping?" Like many theophanies, the meaning is in the inflection. The angels do not need information; they are trying to tell her something with their question.

But Mary is still confused. She, too, thinks of Jesus as a human body. She turns to the man standing before her at the edge of the tomb. He asks the same question as the angels. In her distracted state, Mary can only think of the missing body of her Lord. She confronts the man: "Where have you taken him?"

In what she believed to be the final death, Mary remains faithful in her devotion. She would offer the respect that was custom if she could only find him. Mary does not leave the tomb as the other disciples did, but stays, searches, and questions everyone: "Where is my Lord?"

Then the dramatic, telling moment comes. Jesus says her name: "Mary." And as soon as he does, she recognizes him and responds: "Rabbi." And he sends her out with a message: "Go to the disciples and tell them I am ascending to my God." And Mary Magdalene goes immediately.

There is some significance in what convinced this woman that Jesus stood before her. She does not recognize him by appearance. She does not recognize his voice in his question. What she recognizes is his voice calling her name. When her name is called by the risen Christ, she knows the new truth of the resurrection.

Jesus then makes Mary Magdalene the first evangelist of the resurrection. He sends her out to tell the disciples that he would ascend to God. She does so immediately. Her witness is simple, but profound, in light of the crucifixion: "I have seen the Lord."

In the midst of all the debate about women's place in the church, this story is one of the most significant in the New Testament. Why does John's story show a woman taking the word of the risen Lord? Why is she chosen to be the first to see the risen Christ and the first to be given an explicit mission? It is not extraordinary service that she has come to give. Her consternation involves the change that prevents her from fulfilling her acts of devotion. Mary Magdalene is not doing anything extraordinary; she is going about the tasks that are part of her steadfast devotion to the man Jesus.

This story can certainly speak to us as women today. Traditionally, women are expected to be steadfast, to be there, wherever "there" is, whether at home, at church, or at work; to be available, committed, and devoted to other people. And as contemporary women, we may be busy with many areas of responsibility, and at times so distracted that we mistake Jesus for a gardener over and over again.

We need to make sure we are available to hear our name called by the risen Christ, and to give ourselves the chance to discover our own true mission. After centuries of being told it is not our place, there are some of us who are being called to proclaim the risen Christ, even to those already recognized as disciples.

GUIDED IMAGERY MEDITATION

Find a comfortable and alert posture. Inhale and exhale slowly . . . one . . . two . . . three. Let the daily confusions fall away.

Imagine you are outside. . . . It is very early in the morning. . . . The day is just beginning. . . . Feel the morning air . . . cool and refreshing. . . . A gentle breeze blows around you.

You are walking along a path. . . . You are on this path because you are searching. . . . Perhaps you know just what you are searching for. . . . Perhaps you are only aware of a restless feeling in your life.

Walk along the path aware of a sense of looking for something. . . . It is getting lighter. . . . Suddenly the air seems full of light and you hear your name called . . . listen. . . . Pay attention.

Then it is quiet. . . . Wait and listen once more. . . . A message comes about your search. . . . Listen. . . . What are you called to do?

Dear God,

We confess our confusion and busyness, which cause us to mistake your presence in our lives. Or we cannot feel your presence at all. Be with us in our searches. Grant us patience and steadfastness to listen for the calling of our names and to follow the purposes you have for us. Amen.

13

Lydia, Priscilla, and Phoebe
Steadfast Women

A certain woman named Lydia, a worshiper of God, was listening to us; she was from the city of Thyatira and a dealer in purple cloth. The Lord opened her heart to listen eagerly to what was said by Paul. When she and her household were baptized, she urged us, saying, "If you have judged me to be faithful to the Lord, come and stay at my home." And she prevailed upon us. **(Acts 16:14-15)**

After this Paul left Athens and went to Corinth. There he found a Jew named Aquila, a native of Pontus, who had recently come from Italy with his wife Priscilla, because Claudius had ordered all Jews to leave Rome. Paul went to see them, and, because he was of the same trade, he stayed with them, and they worked together—by trade they were tentmakers. Every sabbath he would argue in the synagogue and would try to convince Jews and Greeks. **(Acts 18:1-4)**

He [Apollos] began to speak boldly in the synagogue; but when Priscilla and Aquila heard him, they took him aside and explained the Way of God to him more accurately. **(Acts 18:26)**

I commend to you our sister Phoebe, a deacon of the church at Cenchreae, so that you may welcome her in the Lord as is fitting for the saints, and help her in whatever she may require from you, for she has been a benefactor of many and of myself as well. **(Romans 16:1-2)**

I n almost any Christian church today, women are over-represented as lay volunteers and under-represented as lay leaders and clergy. Until the suffragists of the nineteenth century initiated the first women's movement in the church, there was little question about the theological mandate for this arrangement. Ironically, that assumption did not stop women from being missionaries all over the globe, or from founding Sunday schools and churches across the frontier. While the official ecclesiology of the church has been captive to the culture of patriarchy, women have diligently carried out the work of Jesus Christ. They must have been reading their Bibles.

Throughout the history of the Christian church, women have not been mere helpmeets to the cause of Christ, but central to the message and mission of Christianity. A too-narrow interpretation of women's place and work in the early church, and the careless proof-texting of a few verses have left the impression that women functioned only in the background of early Christian expansion.

Certainly, the book of Acts and the Pauline writings were transcribed and passed on in a culture of patriarchy. As is evident in the Old Testament, the cultural oppression and invisibility of women make the stories of their leadership all the more impressive. The implications of the stories of Priscilla, Lydia, and Phoebe leave no doubt that women were considered leaders in the early church and that they did not keep silent.

In the story of Lydia, Paul and Timothy travel to Macedonia to the city of Philippi because Paul had a vision of a man pleading for them to come. One Sabbath, Paul reports that they went out of the city to the river where "there was a place of prayer." The implication here is that Jews in Philippi were not allowed to build a place of worship inside the city walls, and so went outside to worship.

There by the river, Paul and Timothy speak to the women who are gathered. This is a unique setting in all of the Pauline writings. It is outside the city, and the only listeners are women. These are not pagan women; on the Sabbath, they have gathered to pray. Apparently, until Paul and Timothy arrive on the scene, the women regularly meet for prayer and conduct their own worship. Their activities are well enough known in the city for Paul and Timothy to go looking for this place on the Sabbath. The women do not follow the apostles; they have already established a place of prayer, and the two men come to them.

One of the women is named Lydia. She is not a native of Philippi; her home is the city of Thyatira, which is southeast across the Aegean Sea from Philippi. But she is now residing along with her household in this Greek city.

Lydia is a "dealer in purple cloth." This implies that she is economically independent. Also, there is no mention in the account of any male family member. She is the head of her household. But Lydia is a shrewd businesswoman. She is a worshiper of God, though we cannot know whether she is Jewish by descent or a convert.

The most important spiritual truth of this story is her conversion: "the Lord opened her heart." Lydia is a powerful woman; she would have to be able to drive a hard bargain in the marketplace in order to support a household in her own name. But she is also a seeker. She shows rare humility for someone who usually operated entirely on her own.

Lydia is the first convert in Asia; after her baptism, she invites Paul and Timothy to stay in her home. They return there later after imprisonment. While the connections are not strong, the overall text of Paul's writings implies that this house church at Lydia's becomes the church of the Philippians.

Priscilla is another woman who becomes, along with her husband Aquila, a co-worker with Paul. Priscilla and Aquila are refugees in Corinth since they have been forced out of Rome by the emperor Claudius. But they have set up a business of tentmaking and Paul joins them.

Priscilla does not fit the traditional model of womanhood as the church has defined it. She has a skill, tentmaking, and works with her husband to support her household.

Until research led to a close examination of all the texts about Priscilla, I had never heard that any woman accompanied Paul on any part of his journey. But along with Aquila, Priscilla makes the trip from Corinth to Ephesus. There is no indication about how long they were there before Apollos came, but Priscilla's faith and charisma were sufficiently recognized that she had no qualms about challenging the theology of a male preacher.

The story of Apollos tells of an eloquent and enthusiastic evangelist who comes to Ephesus and begins to preach in the synagogue. And Priscilla's part in teaching and correcting his message conveys not only that she "preached" about the Way of

God, but also that her understanding and mature faith were influential in mentoring a male preacher.

One other interesting note about Priscilla concerns the number of times she is mentioned in relation to the work of Paul. In Romans 16, Paul commends her as one who risked her life for him. A citation in 1 Corinthians 16:19 refers to the house church that Priscilla and Aquila led. And in the last verse of 2 Timothy, Paul sends his greetings to them through Timothy. Curiously enough, in the six times in which Priscilla and Aquila's names occur, Priscilla's name is first in four citations. Some scholars interpret this to mean that Priscilla was actually seen as the leader of their house church, since the rhetorical style of that day required address to the most prominent person first in a greeting.

Like Lydia, Phoebe's name is unconnected with any male family member. Phoebe's role in the church at Cenchreae is translated variously as officer, deacon, and deaconess. (The use of "servant" in the King James Version is a mistranslation.) The short verses in Romans do not tell us much, but whatever the title, Phoebe is a leader in her congregation. She is well regarded by Paul for her steadfastness in faith and her help to him and others. By allusion, Paul names Phoebe a "saint." By implication, the simple fact that Phoebe is the only one mentioned from her congregation shows how important her leadership was.

But these two short verses have caused great trouble to those who hold to the proof texts about women keeping silence in the church, and the denial of spiritual authority to women. Since there were women deacons in the churches that Paul founded, there is little reason to forbid women ordination as deacons in the church today.

The stories of Lydia, Priscilla, and Phoebe are joined by references to Mary (Acts 12:12), Chloe (1 Corinthians 1:11) and Nympha (Colossians 4:15), who are also described as leading churches in their homes. There are an additional ten women mentioned by name in Paul's greetings in his letters. This preponderance of women serving as leaders and acting as teachers, prophets, and missionaries overwhelms the three proof texts that the church has used to stunt the spiritual gifts of women throughout its history.

Priscilla, Lydia, and Phoebe are the outstanding women in the company of the committed of the New Testament church. They are models of compassionate and trusted women who were faithful to a Christian calling. They are also women who carried financial power for themselves and their house churches. But most importantly, they are recognized as persons whose spiritual authority and power was crucial to the evangelization of their cities and to the growth of the early church.

As women in the church today, with gifts of teaching, exhortation, and preaching, we can know that they are the sisters of our spirits as we carry out our own calling in Christ's name.

GUIDED IMAGERY MEDITATION

Sit quietly. . . . Take a deep, slow breath . . . and another.

Imagine you are seated in a church sanctuary. . . . The pews around you appear empty. . . . You have come for some quiet time . . . out of the confusion of daily routine. . . . You have come to ponder your calling . . . your commitment to a Christian path.

The spirit of Lydia is here to guide you in the use of resources . . . What do you hear when you open your heart?

The spirit of Priscilla is here. . . . What journey is before you? . . . What risk are you called to take in the name of Jesus?

The spirit of Phoebe is here. . . . What form of leadership in the church are you called to at this time?

Now open your heart to the spirits of your biblical sisters. . . . They are here . . . all around you . . . to be with you . . . to sustain you . . . as you go out into the world to share your spiritual gifts with the world and to fulfill the unique mission of Christ that you have been given.

Dear God,

Our lives are very different from those of Lydia, Priscilla, and Phoebe. Most of us are physically comfortable and there is little threat of persecution.

Comfort and safety can make us lazy. Your call to commitment may fall on deaf ears. We may feel threatened by even the idea that we hold spiritual power. We may be scared that others will abandon us or scorn us if we speak and witness out of that power.

When you grant us authority, remind us of Lydia's humility. When you grant us theological insight, remind us of Priscilla's example. When you make a place of leadership for us, empower us to lead out of our hearts and with love.

In the work of worship, tentmaking, and journeying, keep us in the spirit of our biblical sisters. May we join them in the company of the committed. Amen.

Sisters of Woe

14

Eve
Necessary Temptation

Now the serpent was more crafty than any other wild animal that the LORD God had made. He said to the woman, "Did God say, 'You shall not eat from any tree in the garden'?" The woman said to the serpent, "We may eat of the fruit of the trees in the garden; but God said, 'You shall not eat of the fruit of the tree that is in the middle of the garden, nor shall you touch it, or you shall die.'" But the serpent said to the woman, "You will not die; for God knows that when you eat of it your eyes will be opened, and you will be like God, knowing good and evil." So when the woman saw that the tree was good for food, and that it was a delight to the eyes, and that the tree was to be desired to make one wise, she took of its fruit and ate; and she also gave some to her husband, who was with her, and he ate. Then the eyes of both were opened, and they knew that they were naked; and they sewed fig leaves together and made loincloths for themselves.

They heard the sound of the LORD God walking in the garden at the time of the evening breeze, and the man and his wife hid themselves from the presence of the LORD God among the trees of the garden. But the LORD God called to the man, and said to him, "Where are you?" He said, "I heard the sound of you in the garden, and I was afraid, because I was naked; and I hid myself." He said, "Who told you that you were naked? Have you eaten from the tree of which I commanded you not to eat?" The man said, "The woman whom you gave to be with me, she gave me fruit from the tree, and I ate." Then the LORD God said to the woman, "What is this that you have done?" The woman said, "The serpent tricked me, and I ate."   **(Genesis 3:1-13)**

At the Friday night dances after the game in my home-town, I always sensed that the regular preaching against dancing was wrong. Ostensibly the proscription against dancing went all the way back to this story in Genesis. Dancing would inevitably lead to sexual stimulation, and thus to the temptation of sexual love outside of marriage. But pragmatically, I knew that those couples dancing enthusiastically to the latest rock 'n' roll were much less likely to be tempted than the couples wrapped in each other's arms in parked cars just outside the building.

But the proscription and the fears were based in both a misinterpretation of this passage at the very beginning of the biblical story, and in the assumption that sexual sins were the highest order of sin. Adam and Eve's sin is disobedience; the temptation is pride—to be like a god.

Poor Eve and poor us. One bite of forbidden fruit has created a religious tradition that sees only the surface meaning of this passage. And the tradition has led to religious discrimination against women for centuries. Historically, the interpretation given priority is that of Eve as the fallen woman and temptress. Too often, exhortation on this passage describing "the Fall" has limited blame to Eve and does not address the complexity of what tempted Eve.

A later passage notes that Adam named his companion Eve. The name *Eve* means "life." And Eve is called the Mother of us all. She is the mother of Life, which is the knowledge of good and evil. And Eve succumbs to that all-too-human temptation: "You will be like God, knowing good and evil."

It is through life that we come to have the knowledge of good and evil. When we are young, we hear stories of good and evil Bible and fairy tale characters. But parents have a natural inclination to protect their children from the true impact of evil in the world. Adam and Eve were the original innocent children of God, knowing nothing of the evil possible in the world. In the beginning, humans had no moral responsibility. They never had to make ethical decisions about behavior that affects others for good or ill.

But as adults we have learned that there is evil in the world. We know that we are often tempted to do the wrong thing. Or more often, we are tempted by laziness not to do the right thing. We become aware of our own personal power and how close the edge of evil is in our lives.

The serpent's temptation to Eve is not to be evil, but to have knowledge of good and evil—to know as God knows, that there is good and evil in the world. To have knowledge is to have the right to make the choice between being and doing good or doing and being evil. Sometimes these choices are simple. Sometimes determining the right action is very difficult, and it is only by reflection that we realize how close to evil we've come. Or we are confronted by evil when we have actually participated in wrongdoing.

The passage says that the fruit of the tree was "a delight to the eyes." Sin is not accidental; there is always some conscious consideration of behavior and consequences. And this is the point we are all familiar with, whether we admit it or not. We have all faced situations in which we were aware of the temptation to misuse our power. And these situations nearly always involve other persons, who are in some way dependent on us.

Eve shows us our humanness. The temptation she succumbs to is one we all have in some arena of our lives—to be a little like a god; to know more about life than we so far have been given to know. Such "fruit" is tempting to contemplate. It means power, more power than God allows. Such temptation is the denial of our finitude, the limits of any created being. Just like us, for Adam and Eve the sin is spiritual pride; the method is disobedience.

And the threat of God does not come true. After eating, Eve is not struck down, but embarrassed at her nakedness. Her first knowledge of good and evil is of her own body. Most of us have seen the delight of a toddler freed from confining clothes, running around or splashing in a bath. This is the innocence Adam and Eve had before they gave in to the temptation. It is a fresh, unself-conscious wonder that few adults can remember. It is in the awareness of their nakedness that God knows that Adam and Eve have defied the command.

And look again at Adam's response to God's question: "The woman whom you gave to be with me"—it's all her fault. And by implication, Adam blames God since God created his companion. Adam's first words make Eve a scapegoat for his behavior. The first scapegoat in the Bible is the first woman. Adam refuses to acknowledge any personal responsibility for his disobedience.

Adam's first words in relation to his own behavior are: "It is not my fault." Early theologians adopted this theme and argued that because men are sexually tempted by women's bodies, women are responsible for the men's behavior. Adam's excuse, "It is not my fault," has echoed down through the centuries.

Eve does the same by blaming the wily serpent. She cannot resist the idea that her creation by God is more important than her obedience. And she passes this temptation of a god's infinite knowledge of good and evil onto Adam.

These excuses mark a definition of human adulthood for us. Adam and Eve's blame of another is the response of a child. "She made me do it." But before God, and as adults, we learn that our behaviors are our responsibility. If we act so that we are cursed and banned from the garden, we must recognize and accept responsibility for our actions.

I think it is important today to see Eve as much more than the woman who sinned and was blamed by Adam and punished. Her temptation is a part of our life.

Sometimes the church's method is not to teach us to be responsible for our lives and behavior, but instead the elimination of temptation itself. Growing up, I heard many sermons against dancing—as if such teaching could eliminate sexual attraction and expression.

We are given not only life by God, but also the responsibility of choice. We are responsible for our choices and behaviors whatever the consequences. We should neither be made the scapegoats for others' temptations, nor blame others for our own. We can begin by considering Eve's temptation and sin, then reflect on what our own response might be.

GUIDED IMAGERY MEDITATION

Find a comfortable place that allows you to remain alert. Begin breathing slowly and deeply.

Imagine you are in a lush and beautiful garden. . . . The trees are so dense overhead that little light comes in. . . . But the garden is full of flowers. . . . Everywhere you look you see red, yellow, and purple against a background of deep green. . . . Look around. . . . Absorb the beauty.

Slowly you become aware of another presence in the garden. . . . This presence seems sinister. . . . You are uneasy. . . . This sinister presence stands for an area of your life that tempts you right now. . . . What is it?

The temptation is that you will have the knowledge of good and evil. . . . What is it you want to know all things about? . . . What about this temptation is pleasing to contemplate? . . . What happens inside when you consider this power?

Face the temptation for a moment. . . . What do you do?

Dear God,

We don't really want to think about the fact that temptation is a daily part of our lives—that at one time or another, we all want to be gods. We want to believe we are strong in the face of temptation. Confront us with your presence; make us honest and able to acknowledge our pride and desire for power.

When we falter, remind us of your everlasting forgiveness. Amen.

15

Hagar
God's Comfort and Protection

The angel of the LORD found her by a spring of water in the wilderness, the spring on the way to Shur. And he said, "Hagar, slave-girl of Sarai, where have you come from and where are you going?" She said, "I am running away from my mistress Sarai." The angel of the LORD said to her, "Return to your mistress, and submit to her." The angel of the LORD also said to her, "I will so greatly multiply your offspring that they cannot be counted for multitude." And the angel of the LORD said to her,

> "Now you have conceived and shall bear a son;
>   you shall call him Ishmael,
> for the LORD has given heed to your affliction.
> He shall be a wild ass of a man,
> with his hand against everyone,
>   and everyone's hand against him;
> and he shall live at odds with all his kin."

So she named the LORD who spoke to her, "You are El-roi"; for she said, "Have I really seen God and remained alive after seeing him?"

(Genesis 16:7-13)

But Sarah saw the son of Hagar the Egyptian, whom she had borne to Abraham, playing with her son Isaac. So she said to Abraham, "Cast out this slave woman with her son; for the son of this slave woman shall not inherit along with my son Isaac." The matter was very distressing to Abraham on account of his son. But God said to Abraham, "Do not be distressed because of the boy and because of your slave woman; whatever Sarah says to you, do as she tells you, for it is through Isaac that offspring shall be named for you. As for the son of the slave woman, I will make a nation of him also, because he is your offspring." So Abraham rose early in the morning, and took bread and a skin of water, and gave it to Hagar, putting it on her shoulder, along with the child, and sent her away. And she departed, and wandered about in the wilderness of Beer-sheba.

When the water in the skin was gone, she cast the child under one of the bushes. Then she went and sat down opposite him a good way off, about the distance of a bowshot; for she said, "Do not let me look on the death of the child." And as she sat opposite him, she lifted up her voice and wept. And God heard the voice of the boy; and the angel of God called to Hagar from heaven, and said to her, "What troubles you, Hagar? Do not be afraid; for God has heard the voice of the boy where he is. Come, lift up the boy and hold him fast with your hand, for I will make a great nation of him." Then God opened her eyes and she saw a well of water. She went, and filled the skin with water, and gave the boy a drink.

God was with the boy, and he grew up; he lived in the wilderness, and became an expert with the bow.   **(Genesis 21:9-20)**

*H*agar's desert was a literal one. Today, ours are often deserts of the mind or heart. I drove into one on the interstate the day I left a job, after learning of the real reason the environment there had become intolerable. Why had my name been used in a lie? What possible motivation could other professionals have had to stoop so low? One had once been betrayed by male ministers. Was she, like Sarah perhaps, just passing it on? The repercussions lasted for months. Like Hagar, the only choice was to sit in the desert and wait for God.

Hagar's story is one of the dark ones in the Bible. It is a tragic drama of surrogate motherhood with the same ethical dilemmas and personal pain we read about in the newspaper. It is a soap opera of conflict and jealousy between two women and one man. Why is Hagar's story seldom told? Is it just a warning against pride? Or do we have trouble understanding the hard hearts of favorite Old Testament hero and heroine, Abraham and Sarah?

Traditionally, God's promise of a nation through Isaac is seen as the rationale for Hagar's treatment. Imagine the story from Hagar's point of view. She is a slave. Her life is not her own, but Sarah offers Hagar to Abraham out of desperation over her own barrenness. Hagar has no choice. Neither her life nor her body truly belongs to her. Giving birth to Ishmael inevitably raises her status in the family, and her pride gets the better of her. Did she murmur and gossip in the women's quarters about Sarah's emptiness?

It is not a traditional household. Sarah has the power to tell Abraham, "You must answer for my humiliation." And not only does he grant her the right to treat her slave as she would, he later sends one of his sons out into the wilderness when God's word is on Sarah's side.

From the tribe to women's quarters in Arab society to American frontier quilting bees to today's coffee klatches and networking groups, women have banded together for mutual support. What happens when that breaks down? Women need each other for emotional support, but individual needs or shortcomings can break the web as it did between Sarah and Hagar. Rejection or betrayal by women we depend on hurts deeply and bitterness is easy.

Whether we realize it or not, each of us may take the role of either Sarah or Hagar. Their relationship was permanently broken by pride and jealousy, because they did not talk about it. Instead, they let a status and power shift destroy whatever friendship they might have had.

We may never know when we have sent a friend into the desert because of our own confusion and shame. We may not know when our own pride and arrogance have denigrated another. Sarah was left with her status intact within the community. Hagar was banished to the desert with her son and a skin of water.

The scene is full of terror. Sarah stands, arms folded, her chin jutting out, Isaac in her arms. Abraham's face is full of regret as he bids Ishmael good-bye and points the way out to Hagar. In that environment, this action by Sarah and Abraham means certain death for Hagar and Ishmael. And it would most likely be a long, miserable death for both the mother and child. They will be absolutely at the mercy of God in that desert.

This event foreshadows the near sacrifice of Isaac. But in this story, there is no hint of God's initiative. Instead, incredibly, the word of God supports the jealous anger of Sarah. In this case, it is Hagar's previous obedience to the angel's message that is crucial. And even more amazing, this slave girl is given exactly the same promise as the patriarch, Abraham; your descendants will be too many to be counted.

Hagar is called on to risk not only her son's life, but also her own. More is required of her than even of Abraham in order to claim God's promise for the future.

Hagar leaves to wander with Ishmael until the water was gone. Then she thrusts him under a bush; according to the context, Ishmael would have been about fourteen, fully able to understand what was happening, if not why. Surely he began to cry soon after she left. And why did she leave? Was she hysterical? Her rationale is that of every mother who leaves her children: "I can bear it no longer."

But it is at the point of complete desolation and grief that God comes to Hagar for the second time. This time the message is not to return, but is a message of comfort and protection. Hagar finds God and is rescued when she has lost all human community. Once before she had been promised that Ishmael will begin a great nation; she had even named God because of her vision. But this time it is not conditional on her return.

God's word is very practical: "Get to your feet." Getting to our feet is the hard part, but it is the movement out of desolation that changes our point of view. In the paralysis of despair, almost any movement makes a difference. God's command is that Hagar go back to Ishmael, to the one even more vulnerable than she is. She is to go back to the crying child and hold him in her arms. Inexplicably, the requirement is that she comfort Ishmael, who is, along with Isaac, part of the promise of God.

And the story tells us "God opened her eyes." Only after she stands up, tries one more time to follow God's command, and goes back for Ishmael are her eyes opened to the well of water that will save their lives.

Listening for God's voice, getting to our feet, and comforting another are often unimaginable acts in the desert places of our lives. The pain of rejection and abandonment, the anguish of betrayal and loneliness are at times seemingly unbearable. That is because desert experiences can drain us not only of energy, but also of hope.

But Hagar's story is for those desert times in our lives. They are the times when we have been enslaved or betrayed, when we feel expendable because the power structures of our lives seem oblivious to our gifts. Most of all, Hagar's story is for the times when we have been rejected or abandoned and need more than anything to hear God's voice. Because in those times God's presence is required to open our eyes, so that we can see the well that contains the water of consolation, mercy, and assurance.

GUIDED IMAGERY MEDITATION

Find a comfortable, yet alert posture. . . . Breathe deeply and slowly.

There has been an argument. . . . Your ears are full of angry words. . . . You want to talk back . . . tell your side. . . . But you are being sent away. . . . into the desert, which is dry and empty.

You are not alone. . . . Someone you love is with you. . . . You are responsible for this someone. . . . You must take care of them. . . . Name this someone. . . . Your water is all gone. . . . You are both thirsty . . . and desolate. . . . There is no sign of water . . . or rescue. . . . Desperate, you leave your loved one behind . . . and go apart to weep bitterly at the place life has brought you.

And then you hear. . . . "Do not be afraid." . . . A voice promises. . . . God hears you. . . . What do you need God to hear? . . . Hear the words: . . . "Get to your feet." . . . What does that mean in this time?

God will show you life-giving water of mercy and grace. . . . What do you need? . . . Rest in the peace of God's loving providence.

Dear God,

It is our pride that separates us from you, as Hagar was separated from her home. Like Sarah we sometimes misuse our power. Like Hagar we run away from conflict. When we forget you we stubbornly persist until we find ourselves abandoned in the desert. Grant us humility and courage to seek your presence, so that we may know once more the comfort of your steadfast protection. Amen.

16

Sarah
Victimized by Another's Fear

From there Abraham journeyed toward the region of the Negeb,
and settled between Kadesh and Shur. While residing in Gerar as an
alien, Abraham said of his wife Sarah, "She is my sister." And King
Abimelech of Gerar sent and took Sarah. But God came to Abimelech
in a dream by night, and said to him, "You are about to die because of
the woman whom you have taken; for she is a married woman." Now
Abimelech had not approached her; so he said, "Lord, will you
destroy an innocent people? Did he not himself say to me, 'She is my
sister'? And she herself said, 'He is my brother.' I did this in the
integrity of my heart and the innocence of my hands." Then God said
to him in the dream, "Yes, I know that you did this in the integrity of
your heart; furthermore it was I who kept you from sinning against
me. Therefore I did not let you touch her. Now then, return the man's
wife; for he is a prophet, and he will pray for you and you shall live.
But if you do not restore her, know that you shall surely die, you and
all that are yours."

So Abimelech rose early in the morning, and called all his servants
and told them all these things; and the men were very much afraid.
Then Abimelech called Abraham, and said to him, "What have you
done to us? How have I sinned against you, that you have brought
such great guilt on me and my kingdom? You have done things to me
that ought not to be done." And Abimelech said to Abraham, "What
were you thinking of, that you did this thing?" Abraham said, "I did it
because I thought, There is no fear of God at all in this place, and they
will kill me because of my wife. Besides, she is indeed my sister, the
daughter of my father but not the daughter of my mother; and she
became my wife. And when God caused me to wander from my
father's house, I said to her, 'This is the kindness you must do me: at
every place to which we come, say of me, He is my brother.'" Then
Abimelech took sheep and oxen, and male and female slaves, and
gave them to Abraham, and restored his wife Sarah to him. Abimelech
said, "My land is before you; settle where it pleases you." To Sarah he

said, "Look, I have given your brother a thousand pieces of silver; it is your exoneration before all who are with you; you are completely vindicated." Then Abraham prayed to God; and God healed Abimelech, and also healed his wife and female slaves so that they bore children. For the LORD had closed fast all the wombs of the house of Abimelech because of Sarah, Abraham's wife.

(Genesis 20:1-18)

My friend stood in the entry hall of my house, transfixed by the Christmas tree. Her eyes filled with tears. This was her first Christmas as a divorced woman. She had been set aside. After a long marriage, who she really was as a wife had been devalued, then obliterated without her choice. My friend would go through several years of painful self-doubt about her identity and place in the world.

When I went looking for the women of the Bible, I was surprised to find this story of Sarah. Certainly I had never heard the story preached or taught. This must be because it calls into question the celebrated status of Abraham as the faithful patriarch of the twelve tribes.

The whole story of Abraham and Sarah could be written into the script of a soap opera today—"The Days of Our Lives in the Negeb" or "Our Wayward Children of the Promised Land." Traditionally, sermon and Sunday school lesson focus on the call of God, the faithful sojourn, and the miracle of Isaac. The difficulties with Hagar, and this story, as well as Genesis 12:5-20 (a similar story of Sarah as sister), are silenced in the church's teaching.

But this story is significant and instructive to all of us, especially women who have been typecast in the media as "displaced homemakers." Over the last twenty years, increasing numbers of women who have spent decades of their adult lives as committed homemakers suddenly find themselves seeking jobs and careers in order to manage. The emotional roller coaster of divorce is intensified even more by self-doubt and fears about their ability to support themselves and their children. They are additionally victimized by no-fault divorce laws and too many judges who identify with the husband's complaints.

The significant numbers of these women have initiated college courses and employment programs, as special support and training is required to translate the skills learned as homemaker into job employability in the workplace. Like Sarah, these women have been exiled into a strange place, where the rules are difficult to interpret. Like Sarah, in many cases they have been betrayed by a partner's fears.

This particular story falls after the first story of Hagar and the promise of a son to Abraham and Sarah. In the larger context, it is after Sarah laughed at the news of a promised son, then lied about her laughter because she was afraid. Immediately preceding this passage is the strange story of Sodom and Gomorrah and Lot's family. Abraham is "residing in Gerar as an alien." Of course, Sarah is too, but that means different things for the two of them.

Abraham is afraid for his life because apparently under the rule of the land any woman who attracted the king's attention could be taken. A woman had no power or authority over her own life. In the earlier story about Sarah in Pharaoh's household, Sarah is referred to as very beautiful. And, in his defense, Abraham is partially right. Sarah is not his sister, but she is not *only* his wife, either. She is actually the daughter of Abraham's brother, that is, his niece.

Abraham's faith in God's providence fails him. Despite the call to journey and the salvation and covenant he has received in response, Abraham is afraid of the secular rulers. But what of Sarah's sojourn and her required mutual faith in God? Sarah faces these two tests of her faith, and is rescued by God's intervention both times.

Since Abraham has, in effect, handed her over to Abimelech's harem, Sarah is dependent on the wisdom of God's intervention. The method is a dream for Abimelech.

Abraham's fear that Abimelech does not respect God is unfounded. Ironically, it is Abimelech's faith in God's warning, rather than Abraham's faith in God's calling, that saves Sarah. When he confronts Abraham, the only rationale given is Abraham's fear for his own life.

Abimelech's response is almost incomprehensible to us on this side of the Ten Commandments. To the man who has forced his wife into potential adultery, the king gives sheep, cattle, and male and female slaves. Abimelech's relief and gratitude are directed toward Abraham because of God's designation of him as a prophet in a dream. God had given Abimelech a choice: the strange, new, beautiful woman, or his own and his peoples' lives.

Sarah's reputation is worth one thousand silver pieces. Rather than testimony or proof that she is untouched, her chastity is paid for in money. The amount is a huge sum, verifying her beauty and Abraham's public power. Sarah is a nonperson in this story. She only inhabits roles: wife, "sister," and potential concubine to a king. Her value to her community is not based in her personhood or even in her talents. It is only as an unsullied wife that she can return. The thousand pieces of silver are the proof beyond proof of her purity.

This story of Abraham's betrayal of Sarah is another in the Bible in which what is missing is significant. There are no direct words from God other than in Abimelech's dream. Abraham does not attribute any of his own motivation to God's word or leading. And Sarah is silent, just as the church has been silent about this part of her story.

Sarah has had to deny herself to save her husband's life; she has denied her marriage vows, her faithfulness to Abraham, and her own identity, for wife certainly superseded sister. Sarah's place in life, probably her very life, hangs in the balance between these two men—their sense of who they are, and their willingness to listen to God.

Sarah, in her day and time, had no choice at all. The only means for continued life was faith in Abraham and his call from God. But too many women today function in the same mode. All their faith about what life can be is invested in a husband, not in themselves and not in God. And like Sarah, too many of them are betrayed. They are betrayed by physical violence, by alcoholism, and by enforced divorce.

When a woman has been raised to put her faith about life in a husband's hand and she is betrayed or abandoned, she has nothing left. Sarah's story is a warning to us. It is God who should command our faith, not another person. Sarah had no choice, but today women who seek God's providence and who grow their own faith do have a choice.

GUIDED IMAGERY MEDITATION

Find a comfortable position and take a slow, deep breath. . . . Settle your body into the chair. . . . Breathe deeply and slowly.

Imagine you are in a place where you carry out one of your roles. . . . It may be at work . . . or at home . . . or at church . . . or someplace in your community.

You are engrossed in a task for this role. . . . Someone comes in and tells you what has happened.

You have been betrayed. . . . Someone you trusted, someone you had great faith in . . . has used your name and position . . . this person has lied . . . in order to protect himself or herself.

What is your response? . . . Do you feel anger? . . . Are you hurt and sad? . . . Do you consider revenge?

Stop for a moment and think of what you had invested in this person. . . . Have you misplaced your faith?

Stop for a moment in your searching for understanding. . . . God has protection to offer. . . . Imagine the shield you need. . . . Before you act . . . rest in God's protection and love. . . . Trust that your true value will be known. . . . What is that true value? . . . What does your faith in God say about you?

Dear God,

Betrayal by friend or loved one is one of the most painful human experiences. We wonder whether we can dare trust again. If our betrayer has a public Christian reputation, we may nourish revenge as a response, or, like Sarah, pass on the blow to a Hagar in our lives. Reach out to us in these hard and confusing times. Remind us of your providence, which goes beyond what any human can offer. Teach us to wait on your leading, to understand our own value in this world, and to resist revenge. Amen.

17

Daughter of Jephthah
Pride and Pain

Then the spirit of the LORD came upon Jephthah, and he passed through Gilead and Manasseh. He passed on to Mizpah of Gilead, and from Mizpah of Gilead he passed on to the Ammonites. And Jephthah made a vow to the LORD, and said, "If you will give the Ammonites into my hand, then whoever comes out of the doors of my house to meet me, when I return victorious from the Ammonites, shall be the LORD's, to be offered up by me as a burnt offering." So Jephthah crossed over to the Ammonites to fight against them; and the LORD gave them into his hand. He inflicted a massive defeat on them from Aroer to the neighborhood of Minnith, twenty towns, and as far as Abel-keramim. So the Ammonites were subdued before the people of Israel.

Then Jephthah came to his home at Mizpah; and there was his daughter coming out to meet him with timbrels and with dancing. She was his only child; he had no son or daughter except her. When he saw her, he tore his clothes, and said, "Alas, my daughter! You have brought me very low; you have become the cause of great trouble to me. For I have opened my mouth to the LORD, and I cannot take back my vow." She said to him, "My father, if you have opened your mouth to the LORD, do to me according to what has gone out of your mouth, now that the LORD has given you vengeance against your enemies, the Ammonites." And she said to her father, "Let this thing be done for me: Grant me two months, so that I may go and wander on the mountains, and bewail my virginity, my companions and I." "Go," he said and sent her away for two months. So she departed, she and her companions, and bewailed her virginity on the mountains. At the end of two months, she returned to her father, who did with her according to the vow he had made. She had never slept with a man. So there arose an Israelite custom that for four days every year the daughters of Israel would go out to lament the daughter of Jephthah the Gileadite.

(Judges 11:29-40)

The stories became horrifyingly more commonplace in the daily newspaper. A father, depressed by unemployment or enraged by a wife's separation, gets a gun and murders his entire family, and perhaps himself. His word to the world seems to be that he cannot bear the wound to his pride that his family reality presents. What does society do about such situations? Are there any measures to prevent them? These men are wounded, but their actions convey that public appearances and perceptions of their status are more important than the lives of the women and children they claim to love.

The story of Jephthah's daughter is one from the Old Testament that many women have never heard. Since it is the story of Israelite human sacrifice to Yahweh, some scholars place it outside the norm of Israelite history.

Amazingly, some interpreters praise Jephthah's actions. *The Anchor Bible: Judges* describes Jephthah as "an exemplary Yahwist judge" (Doubleday & Company, 1975). *The Interpreter's Dictionary of the Bible* states that his "indomitable will was memorable" (Abingdon Press, 1990). *The Interpreter's Bible*, vol. 2, notes the "daughter's noble submission" and the "power and dignity of an indomitable will" (Abingdon Press, 1981). Curious praise for a story of human sacrifice based on a vow that is not required by God.

Perhaps it is understandable that this story is unfamiliar. Phyllis Trible calls it one of the texts of terror in the Bible. We would rather not look straight into the terror. But it is there in Judges following the family story of Jephthah, an illegitimate son banished by his brothers. And like many of the stories of women in the Bible, their stories begin with the public and private experiences of the powerful men in their lives. His story begins in Judges 11:1. Because he was a bastard, Jephthah's half brothers did not want to share their inheritance and banished him. He formed a band of outlaws and "went raiding" according to verse 3. But he was remembered as a fierce warrior, so when the Israelites were attacked by the Ammonites, he was asked to return to lead them in war. He makes his first bargain by requiring that if he is victorious, he will be recognized as the leader of his people. Initially, Jephthah tries conciliation with his enemies, the Ammonites. When they refuse and he has to go to war, Jephthah makes his vow.

It is important to note here that God does not request this sacrifice, or any sacrifice in exchange for victory. Jephthah makes it voluntarily. As the banished son asked back to lead and conquer, he was in a precarious position. He needed victory over the Ammonites to secure his leadership. Since this bargain is the basis for the tragedy, it is important to look at the words closely.

Jephthah's naïve and tragic vow comes from his anxiety over the battle. His own redemption of his past is at stake. This is not faith in Yahweh. He does not trust that the God of the covenant will deliver his people and redeem him in the eyes of his brothers. So he makes a hasty and ill-conceived bargain with God to try to guarantee victory. Jephthah does not participate in the covenant of faith; he just makes a political bargain. The fatal error of Jephthah's spiritual pride is applying the mode of human power brokering to his relationship with God. His bargain costs him his only daughter.

The tragic scene begins with the daughter's joy. She comes out to meet her victorious father with timbrels and dancing. But Jephthah's response to her welcome is not a noble one. Incomprehensibly, he blames her for his pain: "You have brought me very low; you have become the cause of great trouble to me." This is a classic example of blaming the victim. His daughter could not have known of his vow. Her intention is the purely innocent one of celebration, but in Jephthah's twisted logic—since he cannot accept responsibility for his hasty bargain and lack of faith—someone must be blamed for the tragedy.

His daughter is an obedient girl, raised in a strict patriarchy to do the will of her father. She breaks her silence to acknowledge her obedience, and asserts herself to ask for two months' reprieve to mourn the fact that she will die a virgin. In her culture, to die a virgin meant to die unfulfilled—in essence, to live a life that simply did not count for anything in her family's story. In one of the biblical models that has impacted our culture, an Israelite woman's meaningful existence was based on the bearing of children; and the meaning of her life and identity was based on the accomplishments of her sons.

And she goes away with her companions for two months to prepare herself for the sacrifice—two months mourning that her life would soon end, unfulfilled and incomplete. What was that time like? She took companions with her. They will spend two months in the mountains "bewailing her virginity." We can safely assume that only women went with her. Imagine the sound of women weeping the loss of meaning in one girl's life, weeping for two months, day and night. We are reminded of other stories of women weeping together, such as the account in Jeremiah and Matthew of Rachel mourning the death of innocent children.

The text reports that Israelite women formed the custom of dedicating four days each year to go out from community "to lament the daughter of Jephthah." What does this enigmatic experience signify to women today? Certainly, the magnitude of the loss of all the women and girls destroyed by male violence is worth four days' lament.

Chapter 11 of the book of Judges is the tragic story of a father's spiritual pride and a daughter's unquestioned obedience. Jephthah's daughter had no idea that she might have another option, that her life might belong to her and not to her father. This daughter's sacrifice is not of her own choosing. Her very life is at the mercy of her father's spiritual pride and his public ego. She has to pay with her life for the bargain of his shallow faith.

This is another story that makes us ask: what about the significance of what is missing? Why does Jephthah not question his hasty vow? He apparently never considers going to the mountains himself to seek God's guidance about this tragic outcome. Jephthah is not one to seek God's guidance; he leans completely to his own understanding. His desire to reestablish his public status and his pride cause the death of his daughter.

Today some women have grown to adulthood not realizing that they have choices about the kind and degree of sacrifice they make for another's pride. Some women spend their entire lives in distant hills mourning a symbolic virginity. They have never been given or taken their best time and energy for themselves. The creation of a life, the fulfillment of the incipient whole self inside has never reached full development. The true self inside dies a virgin, and the life they were given to live fully, the life made in the image of God, remains incomplete.

This meditation is designed to allow reflection upon sacrifice that may have been imposed on us, not freely chosen as faithful persons. What has held you down, held you back, made you less than who you really are?

GUIDED IMAGERY MEDITATION

Find a comfortable position and begin taking several deep slow breaths.

Imagine that you have gone to the hills. . . . You are in a place of retreat. . . . You have withdrawn from your daily jobs to spend time alone.

You have set out on a slow, meandering walk through the woods. . . . What season is it? . . . What do you see?

You come to a big sun-warmed rock and sit down to rest. . . . As you look around you notice a young tree . . . a skinny sapling bent in half. . . . The leafy top of the tree is caught under a large, dead limb.

This tree stands for an unchosen sacrifice you have made. . . . Something you've given up to salvage the pride of someone else. . . . Name this sacrifice.

Slowly you stand and walk over to the bent tree. . . . Bend down and move the fallen limb. . . . It is not as heavy as it looks. . . . Move it out of the way. . . . Freed of its burden, the young tree's branches swing up into the air and reach toward the sun. . . . Take a moment to look at it. . . . Now it . . . and you . . . are free to grow.

Dear God,

Change is always uncomfortable. We often take the pain of unchosen sacrifice over the potentially painful risk of being free to choose. Remind us that your love is liberating; your love is not the kind that imposes sacrifice, but one that offers the chance to choose what our sacrifice—in your name—will be. Amen.

Sisters of Courage

18

Shiphrah and Puah
Courageous Creation

The king of Egypt said to the Hebrew midwives, one of whom was named Shiphrah and the other Puah, "When you act as midwives to the Hebrew women, and see them on the birthstool, if it is a boy, kill him; but if it is a girl, she shall live." But the midwives feared God; they did not do as the king of Egypt commanded them, but they let the boys live. So the king of Egypt summoned the midwives and said to them, "Why have you done this, and allowed the boys to live?" The midwives said to Pharaoh, "Because the Hebrew women are not like the Egyptian women; for they are vigorous and give birth before the midwife comes to them." So God dealt well with the midwives; and the people multiplied and became very strong. And because the midwives feared God, he gave them families. **(Exodus 1:15-21)**

O f all significant human events, the birth of a baby is perhaps the most hopeful. One of the reasons for the drama is that, for the mother and the baby, the birth process holds a varying degree of threat. Most of the time, all is well. Sometimes there is tragedy that denies hope. The death of an infant is a unique loss because it is the loss of the future. The birth of a baby is a struggle between life and death.

And the biblical story is built on the stories of births. While historically most of the interpretive work has been done with public events in the Bible, the history of the Israelites and the beginning of Christianity come about through birth. And the early church uses the image of birth to convey what becoming a follower of Jesus means: being "born again" into new life with Christ.

Sarah gives birth to Isaac, and the promise to Abraham of a great nation begins. Rebekah gives birth to Jacob, and the drama intensifies through his struggles. Leah and Rachel, and their maids Bilhah and Zilpah, give birth to sons who become heads of the twelve tribes of Israel. Joseph is carried to Egypt; his brothers and father are brought there because of famine, and we come to the setting of the story of Shiphrah and Puah, the courageous midwives.

The beginning of the book of Exodus reveals that God's promise has come true. The descendants of Abraham and Sarah have become such a great nation that even though they do not live in their native land, they are a threat to the ruler of Egypt. The king ordered that the Israelites be enslaved and put them to the tasks of field labor and making bricks.

But in spite of the ruthlessness of their captors, the Israelite women continued to give birth. The people grew in numbers to such an extent that the king tried genocide.

Imagine the midwives' anxiety and fear. Called before the king of Egypt, Shiphrah and Puah are given a clear mandate. Though they are midwives to lowly slaves, the king has seen them as the key to controlling the Israelites, who are "more numerous and more powerful than we."

The king's ruling goes against everything they had ever done: dedicated to preserving life, they are ordered to destroy it. The next phrase explaining Shiphrah and Puah's actions is a most significant one in the Old Testament: "The midwives feared God; they did not do as the king of Egypt commanded them." Shiphrah and Puah, as midwives, are next in line after the matriarchs and patriarchs of Israelite history to continue the story's revelation. They further God's purposes because they fear God, and because they act out of that reverence.

Shiphrah and Puah defy the king's order by simply going back to their work. They continued to be present and assist the Hebrew women in birth, and to rejoice with the family as each new son or daughter arrived.

Given the situation, the king's reaction seems mild. He doesn't have the midwives murdered immediately, but calls them back to account for their defiance. Certainly, this scene is full of drama. The women stand, unafraid, before the king and his court. They have no obvious power of any kind; they are slaves. But the power they feel and speak and demonstrate is an inner power. It is the fear of God, the trust brought by reverent faith that they are doing what is right in God's eyes, regardless of the political and military powers that can determine their fate.

Shiphrah and Puah have a shrewd answer ready: the Israelite women are "vigorous" and give birth too quickly—even before a midwife is called. The king responds with another order that male children be killed, but Shiphrah and Puah are able to go on with their lives with the knowledge that they have not betrayed the oppressed and innocent infants, whose lives they treasure. The story notes that God rewarded Shiphrah and Puah with homes and families of their own, because they had acted out of their sense of call and the worship of God.

Historically and in our own time, the image of midwife is a very significant one. The midwife is one who assists at the birth and assumes responsibility for both the one giving birth and the new life. This role has always been performed by women, who were crucially important to their community.

During the long night of birth, the midwife is the one called on to keep faith in the miracle, to act on the side of life, not death. The midwife pits all her skills and experience against the threat that this new life and symbol of hope might be lost. She is there, steadfast, not to replace the mother's work, but to support her in the struggle of the labor process.

The creation, the birth of anything new, requires a midwife. Whether it is a new career, an artistic effort, a new discipleship or mission program or community action project, a midwife is needed. We all need people who stand as symbolic midwives in our lives, who are steadfast encouragers to us about what seems too great a struggle, too threatening, too scary. Just like Shiphrah and Puah, our midwives must have faith that they work on the side of God's hope for us.

There are situations and roles for each of us in which we are the midwives at the birth of something or someone. It may be a child's dream, a church or community group project, or our own long-denied creative talent. When we act in the role of midwife, we are mentors, the ones who teach and prod, who support and encourage the creation of something brand new in the world. And in that role we must have faith; we must discern what the new creation could be and our part in it.

Just as birth is a struggle between life and death, the creation of something new is a struggle between tradition and the future, between the possible and the accepted. We may never face the kind or degree of oppression that Shiphrah and Puah faced. But the changes that new birth requires always threaten the status quo, whether it be internal spiritual or psychological change, or a change in a family or church structure. "The way we have always done it," or "our church's policy," or "what I am comfortable with" are the oppressions of civilized society. Just like the king of Egypt's oppression, the inherent resistance of familiarity to change is based on fear of what that change might mean.

And just as for Shiphrah and Puah, the challenge to fear is faith. The midwives feared God above all else. They acted out of their first reverence, the one in their hearts for the God of the promised future. Against that faith and that promise, the oppression of political structure had no chance.

Shiphrah and Puah are examples to us that sometimes the life-protecting role of midwife calls us to defy the secular ruler and fear-based tradition in order to be true to the call of God. To bring in the new creation may very well require defiance of the status quo and shrewd argument with the powers that be. By faith in God, we may thereby support and encourage the new life of those who have been oppressed.

GUIDED IMAGERY MEDITATION

Rest comfortably in your chair. . . . Take a deep breath . . . slowly . . . and another.

Someone has called you. . . . "Come," they say, "and help. . . . We need your help with this new wonderful thing that is happening." . . . What is it? . . . What are you going to help come to life?

It will not be easy. . . . As with all births, there is a struggle.

Then another call comes. . . . You are summoned to judgment. . . . The judge says, "You must stop. . . . You cannot go on with this creation." . . . What do you say?

Return to the place of new creation. . . . You may be criticized or lose status or acceptance if you go on. . . . What now? . . . What will you do?

Who has claim on your first reverence?

Summoned once again to the public judge, what response do you make?

For your faith and courage, claim the promise that God will provide for you.

Dear God,

Birth of any kind is difficult and commands all our attention. Most of the time we want to put aside the responsibility and say, "Not me, Lord." Give us the courage and shrewdness of Shiphrah and Puah. Make our hearts strong and our hands ready as we midwife something new in this world. Amen.

19

Ruth
Courage to Risk

But Naomi said to her two daughters-in-law, "Go back each of you to your mother's house. May the LORD deal kindly with you, as you have dealt with the dead and with me. The LORD grant that you may find security, each of you in the house of your husband." Then she kissed them, and they wept aloud. . . . Then they wept aloud again. Orpah kissed her mother-in-law, but Ruth clung to her.

So she said, "See, your sister-in-law has gone back to her people and to her gods; return after your sister-in-law." But Ruth said,

> "Do not press me to leave you
> or to turn back from following you!
> Where you go, I will go;
> Where you lodge, I will lodge;
> your people shall be my people,
> and your God my God.
> Where you die, I will die—
> there will I be buried.
> May the LORD do thus and so to me,
> and more as well,
> if even death parts me from you!"

When Naomi saw that she was determined to go with her, she said no more to her.

So the two of them went on until they came to Bethlehem. When they came to Bethlehem, the whole town was stirred because of them; and the women said, "Is this Naomi?"   **(Ruth 1:8-9, 14-19)**

T he book of Ruth is unique in the Bible for two reasons. The first, of course, is that the main characters are women, and the story is told from their point of view.

The second is that the content of the story is human relationships. This book of God's revelation does not have a political or military aspect. The entire message is both about and disclosed through the relationship of two women. The significance of the book in the biblical canon involves an important genealogy. Through Ruth's loyalty to Naomi, they both return to Judah, Ruth marries Boaz, and the historical line from Judah to David is kept intact.

But even without the historical significance, this is a wonderful story about a woman's courage, dedication, and willingness to take a risk. The background of Ruth's story is anything but auspicious. Elimelech was from Bethlehem in Judah, and because of famine there he takes his wife and sons to Moab. The sons marry Moabite women. Ruth's ancestry would likely have been a source of shame to the Israelites. Moab was the son of Lot and his eldest daughter, according to Genesis 19. But in time of famine there was no assurance of return to Judah, and the primary requirement was that the sons take wives to maintain the family line—even if that meant foreign wives.

But tragedy befalls the family when Elimelech and both his sons die. Their deaths make Naomi the foreign woman in the land of Moab, with no economic security or status. For her, the return to Bethlehem, the land of her people, is the only possible means of survival.

Initially Ruth and Orpah start out with Naomi. But then Naomi sends them back to their mothers' houses with the blessing that they find new husbands and security. At first they both protest, but Naomi's argument that there will be no sons from her for them to marry convinces Orpah. Naomi is being practical; both their physical survival and social status require husbands, which their mothers could seek for them.

But Ruth will not leave her mother-in-law. Her vow is not simple loyalty to a woman who has come to mean a great deal to her. Ruth's pledge is a commitment to another woman against and in the face of all the social structure and custom that most likely will condemn her to poverty as a foreign woman in a strange land. Her personal relationship with her mother-in-law is more important than her own fate. Ruth makes this decision to follow Naomi against Naomi's own advice, against

Orpah's example, and against the logical argument that there are and will be no sons from Naomi to marry. If Naomi is right, Ruth will be abandoned as a childless foreign widow in Judah after Naomi's death. Naomi's family will have no obligation to her.

There is nothing to compare to Ruth's vow to Naomi elsewhere in the Bible. Ruth makes her vow, not because of a theophany, but because of relationships. She makes her vow to follow Naomi's God because of her relationship to Naomi. She makes it outside of blood, nuclear family, or national ties. Ruth attaches her fate to Naomi's simply because of what this woman has come to mean to her, because of the relationship they have with each other.

It is also amazing that the relationship here is daughter-in-law to mother-in-law. In the tradition of most cultures revealed in stories and jokes, these two women should have been adversaries. The stereotypical relationship is competitive: to determine which woman is to be first in the son and husband's affections. But, as often happens in biblical stories, it is the unexpected or unusual that teaches us. The other curious aspect of this vow is the use that has been made of it in traditional wedding ceremonies. Thus a heartfelt vow from one woman to another is transposed into a vow from a wife to a husband.

Such is the relationship between these two women, that out of grief grows a mutual dedication. This mutual dedication allows them to survive in a land where Ruth must essentially be sent out to beg. Without husbands, they have no status or property.

Ruth goes humbly to the fields of Boaz. When Boaz inquires about her, he is told of her devotion to Naomi, his kinswoman. Boaz responds favorably to this foreign woman he discovers in his field, because he admires the risk she has taken to stay with Naomi. Boaz establishes himself as a respectful protector of Ruth and offers a blessing of God's reward upon her.

Another theme in this conversation and in a later one with Naomi is the sexual threat to Ruth as a foreign woman gathering in the fields. Boaz admonishes her to stay close to the young women and to keep her eyes on the field. He even makes the point that he has ordered the young men not to harass her. And

Naomi repeats the recommendation that she stay with the young women in one field. Apparently a young foreign widow was a fair target for sexual advances in the eyes of the men servants. So Ruth is warned to stay with the women and "not raise her eyes." This warning is also probably designed to make certain that there can be no question about Ruth's chastity in case of future marriage.

Naomi may be a bitter woman, but she is not naïve. She is familiar with the marital customs of her country. So when she discovers whose field Ruth gleans, and that Ruth has found favor with Boaz, she instructs Ruth in what may seem like a plot for the seduction of the rich landowner. Ruth is to go to the threshing floor and lie at the feet of Boaz. Whatever we may imagine actually happened, the symbol of Ruth's action is that she is choosing Boaz, asking him by her behavior to fulfill the role of next of kin.

In the Israelite custom, this means that due to Naomi's widowhood, one of her kinsmen has the responsibility of marrying Ruth in order to carry on Elimelech's family line. The situation is somewhat similar to the story of Tamar and Judah told in Genesis 38 (though the ethic of the men involved are totally opposite). The women in both situations initiate sexually implicit behavior, which conveys to the men their cultural obligation. Curiously enough, these two women, who might be seen as sexually aggressive, are mentioned in Matthew's genealogy of Jesus.

Boaz reveals his personal ethic by going to one man who might have closer claims to both Elimelech's land, and ostensibly, to Ruth. The offer of first rights is refused and the other kinsman pledges his relinquishment to Boaz in front of ten witnesses. Boaz makes his claim in public before the elders and the people.

This is followed by an unusual blessing. The people offer a blessing to Boaz and Ruth by calling on the names of Rachel and Leah because they, along with their maidservants, were the mothers of the twelve tribes of Israel. In addition, they are blessed in the name of Perez and Tamar, the ancestors of Boaz, six generations back in his family line. In a story about women and relationships, the public blessing is not given by the male elders and priests, but by the people. And the blessing is not in the name of the patriarchs, but the matriarchs of Israel, including one who played the role of prostitute in order to maintain the line of Judah.

Ruth and Boaz marry and she bears a son. Here another matriarchal element comes in. The women of the tribe bless Naomi. They declare that Ruth, the foreign daughter-in-law, is worth more to Naomi than seven sons. This is the highest praise that the women could give Ruth. Her devotion to Naomi and her willingness to follow Naomi's wisdom have redeemed Naomi's status. She is not condemned to live as a poor beggar among her own people, but has the status of grandmother.

Finally, it is very significant that the women name the son Obed. He will be David's grandfather. Is this detail a foreshadowing of Elizabeth and Mary's relationship and of the power of naming that they hold? Contrary to the assumed patriarchal custom, the important women in Jesus' genealogy name their sons, as did Rachel and Leah.

The story of Ruth and Naomi is the fulcrum story of women in the Bible. It is the telescope through which the stories of women in Israelite history are connected to the stories of women in Jesus' life and gospel. And it is a story of one woman's commitment to another.

Both radical, separatist feminists and traditional, conservative interpretations of biblical women denigrate the significance of women's contribution to the biblical story. What they see as mere threads of obscure stories become in this story a strong cable linking the matriarchs, Rachel and Leah, to the story of a young Hebrew girl, Mary, who said yes to God.

More than anything, this story celebrates Ruth's courage and dedication. It is her willingness to risk her own personal future and be loyal to her mother-in-law that allows their relationship to flourish, and finally provides security for both of them. Ruth and Naomi and their caring for each other are a model of sisterhood to us today.

And the message to us is that security—true security—lies only on the far side of risk. Often it is through our dedication to other women that we find a deep and significant purpose for our lives.

GUIDED IMAGERY MEDITATION

Find a comfortable, yet alert posture. Begin breathing deeply until you feel a sense of peaceful waiting.

Imagine you are standing by the side of a road. . . . Look at the vista around you . . . the sky . . . the land. . . . You are aware that soon a woman will be coming down the road toward you. . . . It may be someone you know . . . or someone who is a symbol of something important to you. . . . Think of who this woman is.

As the woman approaches you are aware that you have a chance to meet her on the road and go with her. . . . The road leads to what is a far country in some area of your life. . . . You feel some fear. . . . What is this far country in your life right now? . . . What is the risk you face?

The woman is near you. . . . As you look toward her, you are aware of a sense of purpose . . . of a challenge to grow. . . . She holds out her hand and invites you to join her on the journey. . . . What might you gain if you go? What might you lose? . . . Make your decision.

Dear God,

We know, but don't want to remember, that anything worthwhile means taking a risk. We do not always feel courageous when we need to. Sometimes we try to ignore the challenges of our lives. Grant us openness to the infusion of your courage in our hearts. Remind us that the challenges of the far country are invitations to grow in your purpose for us. Amen.

20

Mary, the Mother of Jesus
The Hardest Words

In the sixth month the angel Gabriel was sent by God to a town in Galilee called Nazareth, to a virgin engaged to a man whose name was Joseph, of the house of David. The virgin's name was Mary. And he came to her and said, "Greetings, favored one! The Lord is with you." But she was much perplexed by his words and pondered what sort of greeting this might be. The angel said to her, "Do not be afraid, Mary, for you have found favor with God. And now, you will conceive in your womb and bear a son, and you will name him Jesus. He will be great, and will be called the Son of the Most High, and the Lord God will give to him the throne of his ancestor David. He will reign over the house of Jacob forever, and of his kingdom there will be no end." Mary said to the angel, "How can this be, since I am a virgin?" The angel said to her, "The Holy Spirit will come upon you, and the power of the Most High will overshadow you; therefore the child to be born will be holy; he will be called Son of God. And now, your relative Elizabeth in her old age has also conceived a son; and this is the sixth month for her who was said to be barren. For nothing will be impossible with God." Then Mary said, "Here am I, the servant of the Lord; let it be with me according to your word." Then the angel departed from her.   **(Luke 1:26-38)**

I was just supposed to read Scripture and pray on that September Sunday morning. I could not have anticipated what the Holy Spirit had in mind. At the end of his sermon, my pastor turned to me and asked what my "other" name was. In front of the whole congregation, mind you! Caught completely by surprise, I said, "Maurine" because it is also my mother's middle name. My pastor responded, "Mary Maurine Zimmer, you are beloved of God."

I sat stunned by this announcement while the pastor stepped

down to the congregation to repeat the litany for several other members sitting near the front. The experience gave me a hint of what Mary must have felt in Gabriel's presence. She was never again the same. Neither would I ever again be the same.

Have you noticed that we don't talk about angels much anymore? Is it because we fear others' judgment? Or because, given what angels told Mary and others, we would frankly just rather not hear what they have to say? Is it possible that we dread the responsibility of carrying the Christ that such annunciation brings?

Mary was "deeply troubled," or "much perplexed," or "greatly troubled," according to various translations. No matter which translation we use, the effect was the same. Mary was speechless at the appearance, alternately scared and curious, given Gabriel's next words.

My inherent nosiness served me well as a social worker, and I must confess I would like to know what else transpired in that conversation. Is "deeply troubled" a euphemism for a Hebrew teenager's smart response, such as, "You are out of your everloving mind, dear Gabriel"?

Perhaps Mary was a more reticent child, and thus, "deeply troubled" might convey doubt. Or perhaps at first Mary tried to dispel this overwhelming perception by labeling it delusion: "This can't be happening to me!"

For centuries of doctrinal dispute the focus of this story has been on Mary's recorded question: "How can this be, since I am a virgin?" But it is not the happenstance of Mary's state of being that is most significant in our discipleship. The significance is her response, her choice to accept the annunciation, fearful and inexplicable as it might be. She will accept that the "power of the Most High will overshadow" her.

Mary's story is so familiar that we tend to reread it every year and pass over its implications, assuming that the angel's message was unique to one Jewish girl, limited in space and time. Mary's gladsome willingness to serve God at the risk of her betrothal and ostracism from her community is a dramatic, significant example to us of what God's call means.

But the angel's words are significant to us today, also. What this news symbolizes is the gift of the unknown of God in our lives. Something holy is born within each of us according to the New Testament and contemplative writers. Whenever God presents a new challenge—whenever we are "overshadowed," we are in the same state of innocence that Mary was long ago. We don't know what will happen. We don't have a clue as to exactly what our acceptance will mean.

The stage was set for Mary's response—and it is unequivocal: "Here am I, the servant of the Lord; let it be with me according to your word." Mary's response is so simple that it reverberates with meaning. "Here am I." This sounds easy, but it is the hardest response for any of us to make, because we face the same risks that Mary did. Responding to the gift of God's unknown in our life in covenant and redemption history has nearly always meant the chance of social ostracism, political threat, even injury.

Remembering those significant times in our lives when we felt overshadowed and wondered about the meaning of our experience can easily put us in touch with Mary's fears and confusion. The time when you thought: I love him and want to marry him. When you decided: yes, I am going to take that new job or church position. Or when you knew, deep inside: yes, I am a writer, or musician, or artist. Or when the doctor said, "Here is your newborn child." And along with real terror, you felt deep within you the fluttering of new life, of new growth. And you felt washed with blessing—excited, challenged, and scared all at the same time.

Mary does what every sensible woman would. She goes for consultation to someone she knows and trusts, who is a little further along than she. It is too much to expect that Luke would record the details of two pregnant women talking—"Does cooking fish make you gag?" "Just wait until your ankles swell everyday." "I am so scared."

The one detail that we have is that Mary stayed for three months. And the next strand of the story is in Bethlehem at the time of birth.

What about the six months in between? Women in the church today who are standing up, questioning the historical assumptions of the church, and speaking about a change for women know about that six months. We know because we are living in that time between the quickening—the flutter deep inside—and the birth of Christ. We are feeling all those vulnerable feelings, alternating between fear and joy.

Mary's family and community reaction to her situation both at the beginning and throughout her pregnancy can easily be imagined. Joseph has his very own visitation with an angel and his own struggle to say yes to God. But he does the right thing by Mary, though the young couple most likely did not avoid the whispers and sidelong glances of curious and judgmental people. They probably lived quiet, even hidden lives.

And even through the beginning of this century, married, pregnant women were cloistered at home. The obvious evidence of human sexuality had to be hidden. And still today, children born to unmarried women are referred to as "illegitimate." Society still needs foster and boarding homes for pregnant girls whose families cannot bear the reality of their condition.

So it is with our witness as activist women in the church today. Some people, even some of our sisters, wish we would hide ourselves, or at least keep silent.

But if we do, then we are committing what Susan Nelson Dunfee calls the "sin of hiding." With Carol Gilligan, she examines the tragic juxtaposition of selfhood and self-denial for women reared in traditional cultures. To deny self, to hide the self, has been held up as the goal of virtuous Christianity.

But for women, this means we hide the image of God that we are. We deny the Christ that is in us, and by so doing, we are called virtuous by our culture. We end up having to choose between our own spiritual response to God's call and the affirmation of our community.

The sin of hiding is just as much a denial of God as the sin of arrogant pride. It is a rejection of the spirit of compassionate love given to us by God in Christ. To commit the sin of hiding is to reject the fruits and gifts of the spirit that God has formed in us since we were known in the womb.

To come out of hiding is risky, just as Mary's response was risky. To take the light within out from under the basket, and set it on the stand in front of our church and our world is to risk some loss of community. It is to risk the cold wind of ostracism, and to know that we will spend much time looking to our Gabriels, Josephs, and Elizabeths for reassurance and solidarity.

When you are frightened at the awesomeness of your call, try to remember a teen-age Hebrew girl, told what Mary was told and anticipating the loss of community when she shared her truth with them. That is, to different degrees and in different ways, what we risk when we say to God, "Here am I."

The poet Emily Dickinson has some phrases for this moment of annunciation when the angel has proclaimed God's overshadowing. To face it, rather than to run away, is to volunteer to "dwell in possibility" and to realize that possibility dwells in you. This is the unknown of God. And believe it or not, this sense of possibility, of potential, is the source of hope. Hope doesn't come from what we already know, from what is familiar. Sometimes God breaks in and requires us to focus on this potential within, on new and unknown possibilities of the Spirit's gifts to us. Emily Dickinson describes it thus:

Baptized before without the choice,
But this time consciously, of grace
Unto supremest name,
Called to my full. . . .
But this time, adequate, erect,
With will to choose or to reject.
(from *Poems by Emily Dickinson,* ed. Martha D. Bianchi and Alfred L. Hampson)

Even in the between times, we dwell in possibility. And we have the chance once more to say, "Here am I."

GUIDED IMAGERY MEDITATION

Please find a comfortable position. . . . Close your eyes and begin to breathe deeply . . . and . . . slowly.

Imagine you are at home. . . . You have been busy with daily tasks . . . cleaning . . . cooking . . . making phone calls.

It is time to rest. . . . Imagine your favorite place to sit . . . and relax into it. . . . Listen to the silence. . . . Feel the solitude.

Inside you there is possibility. . . . It is the light of Christ . . . that has chosen you . . . and you . . . have in return chosen this gift . . . with your life.

Is any part of it hidden? . . . If so . . . take a minute to look for it . . . What do you find? . . . If you feel uneasy or notice a fear . . . just rest with it for a moment.

Listen to the words. . . . Blessed are you with all women. . . . The Holy Spirit has come upon you. . . . You are bearing the child of God who is your self . . . a unique image of Christ in the world . . . What is your response?

Dear God,

We confess we are often tired, God. Tired of the same battles, the struggle within and the struggle without. Bearing and birthing our inner selves is a labor that takes years.

Show us our need for quiet communion with you. Teach us to find solitude, that we may hear again your promises, new and clear.

Show us the path of our servanthood, that we may tell out your greatness and rejoice in your tender, blessed salvation. Amen.

21

The Canaanite Woman
Getting Needs Met

Jesus left that place and went away to the district of Tyre and Sidon. Just then a Canaanite woman from that region came out and started shouting, "Have mercy on me, Lord, Son of David; my daughter is tormented by a demon." But he did not answer her at all. And his disciples came and urged him, saying, "Send her away, for she keeps shouting after us." He answered, "I was sent only to the lost sheep of the house of Israel." But she came and knelt before him, saying, "Lord, help me." He answered, "It is not fair to take the children's food and throw it to the dogs." She said, "Yes, Lord, yet even the dogs eat the crumbs that fall from their masters' table." Then Jesus answered her, "Woman, great is your faith! Let it be done for you as you wish." And her daughter was healed instantly. **(Matthew 15:21-28)**

At the end of the autobiographical book and movie, *Out of Africa,* Karen von Blixen has lost everything. She has immigrated to South Africa to join her new husband in a farming venture. She has suffered illness and infertility resulting from his infidelity. The harvested coffee crop, which was her last chance to save the farm, has been destroyed in a fire. But she has formed a mutual devotion with the Kikuyu, a native tribe whose members made her farm a possibility. Burdened by the threat that they may lose any chance of remaining on the land, she goes to petition the new governor at a reception being held in his honor. When she is introduced, Karen kneels at his feet to beg for land for the Kikuyu. The governor is mortified with embarrassment. He urges her to stand as the sedate British crowd is politely, but obviously appalled by her behavior. But she is desperate and continues to plead until the governor's wife gives her a nod.

Karen von Blixen and the Canaanite woman have this in common: they are so desperate that they see no other option but the one that risks public humiliation. They are both outsiders in the community of the crowd in the scene; they are "other," because their nationality is different from those whom they petition. They are both disruptive, uppity women in the eyes of those who watch their desperate acts and hear their heartfelt words.

In the context of Matthew's story, Jesus has just been healing people and arguing with the Pharisees; his disciples have warned him that the Pharisees are angry with him and they have once again been a little dense in the head and require Jesus to explain a parable. So perhaps we should give the humanity of Jesus the benefit of the doubt. It has been a stressful time. But his initial response to ignore the anxious, pleading woman is completely out of character. Jesus got angry more than once, but never flatly refused to minister to those who came to him.

The Canaanite woman recognized that they are of different tribes. She is respectful, even in her state of anxiety, calling him "Lord" each time she addresses him. At first Jesus just ignores this loud, foreign woman. The disciples are not gracious; they ask him to "send her away, for she keeps shouting after us."

Maybe, in a backhanded sort of way we should pity the disciples. They did not have psychiatry's traditional name for this woman. Today we would call any woman who comes into our sanctuaries shouting for healing, "hysterical." But just as we recover the Canaanite woman as sister, so also we recover the word *hysteria* and the dramatic implications of its meaning. The word *hysteria* means "weeping of the womb"; it refers to women's cycle of reproduction. And, ironically, almost unbelievably, if it were not for Sarah and Mary's "hysteria," the weeping of their wombs, we wouldn't have a religion, a chosen people, a Savior, or a faith.

When Jesus answers her, his response is exclusionary: "I was sent only to the lost sheep of the house of Israel." His resistance only makes the Canaanite woman more determined; she falls at his feet and begs "Lord, help me." Jesus tries a metaphor, something surely a woman who seeks healing for her daughter will understand. His bread, sustenance for life, is for the chosen people, the children of Israel.

And here we get the full force of the racial enmity that existed between Israelites and Canaanites since the conquest of Canaan. Her people are dogs, compared to Yahweh's chosen ones. This conflict is not solved here; it continues into the early church.

The Canaanite woman has abandoned public pride; she has only her wits left. But they serve her well. Her quick wisdom is to argue that she is not even asking for the children's bread; as an outsider, she does not hope to get the best part of the loaf, or even the heel. Just the crumbs will do. If Jesus will only give her some of what is left over from his ministry to the house of Israel, that will be enough healing for her daughter on this one day.

This is the Canaanite woman's leap of faith—that this man called "Messiah" by some will recognize her devotion to her daughter and her courage to find healing for her. And he does. Marveling at her faith, Jesus tells her that she will receive what she asks. And her daughter is healed.

The Canaanite woman reveals to Jesus that his ministry is needed by all, not just the chosen people. She widens his ministry, throws open the door to the whole world, not only to those who have known to search for a Messiah.

This biblical woman's story is another of the short vignettes of an anonymous foreign woman. With these stories, we must look closely, probing deeply so that we can glean much from a short conversation. We need to get to know the Canaanite woman well, for we will have to keep arguing on behalf of those who are still locked away from the church's healing balm.

Have you ever been an outsider, an "other" in your own church? Have you been so desperate on behalf of another that you could not be silent anymore no matter what embarrassment you might risk? Have you ever been present when a woman the world and even the church might call "hysterical" comes to speak out, to advocate, even to demand healing?

For the Canaanite woman does not speak for herself, but for a sick daughter. Who is the sick child for each one of us? What excluded, abandoned group of people do we advocate in a system that seems to say: "You're too noisy, you make us uncomfortable. Go away."

The statistics are unnerving. One in four adult women, and one in six adult men are survivors of childhood sexual abuse.

One in four women will experience sexual assault sometime in her life. One in two women will either be physically battered by a man who claims to love her or threatened with physical abuse. Even women already in the church are not immune from these statistics.

The Canaanite woman is the original assertive woman. She is assertive to the point of risking being offensive in the original meaning of the word: she continues to strike against those who would exclude her daughter from Jesus' healing powers. She keeps knocking on the door of Jesus' understanding of who he is. And when the door opens, it opens both ways. The door of healing ministry is opened to the despised, foreign child who needs it. And the definition of ministry is widened—it will be for all people.

The proclamation of our lives are these swinging doors. Some of us have been excluded. As women in the church today, we are too often outsiders in different ways and to different degrees. We have a whole history of womanhood to bring to the church today, to represent and thus convey "otherness." We bring the outsiders, whom the church has heretofore too often abandoned, sent away, ignored, or ostracized. We are still in the church, so we can open the door to those who need the church's ministry. Without people who need healing, the church has no ministry of healing.

How we handle the doors of our witness as disciples determines how open the church is. We will have to be persistent. Our knocks at the church doors on behalf of those excluded will have to be strong and clear and steady. We have been promised that if we keep knocking, the door will be opened. Then the invisible, suffering women, men, and children on the outside can make contact with the healing strength that should never be imprisoned behind a door marked "Chosen people."

GUIDED IMAGERY MEDITATION

Find a comfortable, yet alert position. . . . Take a slow, deep breath . . . and another . . . and another.

You are walking down a hallway in a church building. . . . What do you hear? . . . What do you notice about your surroundings?

Your mind and heart are heavy . . . You have just come from a conversation with someone who feels rejected by the church. . . . The person is a member of a group that is not generally accepted by your church. . . . The person is in great emotional pain because of this exclusion. . . . Name the person . . . name the group.

You come to the meeting room . . . and go in. . . . The discussion in the room is about the group that seeks the church's ministry. . . . Faces in the group of church leaders are anxious and serious.

You stand . . . begin to speak. . . . You must speak for inclusion. . . . The group murmurs . . . One woman says loudly . . . "Not in my church."

What do you say? . . . What is your quick wisdom? . . . What sustenance do you seek for those who seek the church's open, healing arms?

Dear God,

Forgive us when we are passive or timid about those on the outside of the church. Bless the quick-witted, assertive woman in each of us who trembles even as she dares. Open our spirits to your strength. Infuse us with the power of your love. Lead us to the ones who need the healing balm of a Christian community. Show us the door we are to knock on for their sake. Amen.